A Pocket Guide to Writing in History

A Pocket Guide to Writing in History

FIFTH EDITION

Mary Lynn Rampolla

Trinity (Washington) University

Bedford / St. Martin's   Boston ◆ New York

For Bedford/St. Martin's
Executive Editor for History: Mary Dougherty
Director of Development for History: Jane Knetzger
Developmental Editor: Katherine A. Retan
Production Editor: Kristen Merrill
Production Supervisor: Andrew Ensor
Executive Marketing Manager: Jenna Bookin Barry
Text Design: Claire Seng-Niemoeller
Cover Design: Hannus Design Associates
Composition: Karla Goethe, Orchard Wind Graphics
Printing and Binding: Malloy Lithography

President and Publisher: Joan Feinberg
Editorial Director: Denise B. Wydra
Director of Marketing: Karen Melton Soeltz
Director of Editing, Design, and Production: Marcia Cohen
Managing Editor: Elizabeth M. Schaaf

Library of Congress Control Number: 2006926011

Manufactured in the United States of America.

1   0   9   8   7

f   e   d   c

For information, write: Bedford/St. Martin's, 75 Arlington Street, Boston, MA 02116 (617-399-4000)

ISBN-10: 0–312–44673–X
ISBN-13: 978–0–312–44673–4

Acknowledgments

Excerpts from the Public Broadcasting Service's *American Experience* documentary, "Monkey Trial," written by Christine Lesiak. Reprinted by permission from WGBH Educational Foundation. Copyright © 2003 WGBH/Boston.

Excerpts from *The Scopes Trial: A Brief History with Documents,* edited with an introduction by Jeffrey P. Moran. Copyright © 2002 by Bedford/St. Martin's.

From *Summer for the Gods* by Edward J. Larson. Copyright © 1997 by Edward J. Larson. Reprinted by permission of Basic Books, a member of Perseus Books, L.L.C.

Online library catalog homepage, Sister Helen Sheehan Library, used with permission of Trinity (Washington) University.

Overhead view of the Scopes trial image © Bettmann/CORBIS.

Preface

A Pocket Guide to Writing in History covers the reading, writing, and research skills students need in order to write effective history papers. Though many students in under-graduate history courses understand that college papers must do more than restate information gleaned from lec-tures and books, they may have only a vague idea of how to go about researching, writing, and documenting a his-tory paper. Instructors, for their part, must convey a great deal of information about history and historical method-ology in a limited amount of time, often in large lecture classes; thus, they can devote only very limited time to writing instruction. *A Pocket Guide to Writing in History* is designed to aid the instructor and provide guidance for the student in just such situations.

Like the four earlier versions, this new edition of *A Pocket Guide to Writing in History* is brief and can be tucked into a pocket or backpack. It maintains the most valuable features of earlier versions, providing thorough coverage of the conventions for writing in history — from analyz-ing an assignments to conducting research, writing an ef-fective paper, avoiding plagiarism, documenting sources, and editing for clarity and style. Models — including sample assignment and sample pages from a research paper — illustrate each step of the research and writing process, and more than ninety annotated documentation models based on *The Chicago Manual of Style* show stu-dents how to cite print, electronic, and nonwritten sources.

This fifth edition has been revised and reorganized to provide more practical help with basic skills as well as new coverage of sophisticated critical-thinking skills — making it more useful for students at all levels.

- New "Tips for Writers" boxes throughout the book highlight key topics such as evaluating sources, reading critically, crafting a strong thesis, and avoiding plagiarism, making it easy for students to locate the advice they need to succeed in their courses.

- Coverage of important whole paper topics such as crafting a thesis statement, drafting a strong introduction and conclusion, and writing clear and connected paragraphs has been expanded and consolidated so students can find the advice they need without flipping between chapters.
- New coverage of the connection between critical reading and effective writing teaches students helpful strategies for approaching writing assignments that rely on their ability to read critically — such as annotated bibliographies, book reviews, and historiographic essays.
- A new section on crafting a strong argument teaches students how to use evidence to support a thesis and how to anticipate counterarguments.
- A new section on developing a research plan and an expanded section on conducting research give students thorough advice on how to use a variety of print and electronic resources to locate reliable historical sources and how to enter the Web through a good portal such as a gateway site or on-line journal archive.
- The appendices highlight the most recent and helpful indexes, references, periodicals, and Internet sources as places for students to start their research.

In working on this edition, I profited from the advice and encouragement of my colleagues at Trinity (Washington) University, especially my colleagues in the History program. I owe special thanks to the students in my Fall 2005 senior seminar who served as "guinea pigs" for many of the new "Tips for Writers" boxes and who offered feedback throughout the semester on new and revised sections of the text. I am especially indebted to the following historians who reviewed the fourth edition and offered extremely helpful suggestions in preparation for the fifth edition: John R. Buschmann, Community College of Aurora; Colleen A. Donlavy, University of Wisconsin–Madison; Jennifer L. Gross, Jacksonville State University; Janet G. Hudson, Winthrop University; Anthony Iaccarino, Reed College; Ben Lowe, Florida Atlantic University; Shulamit Magnus, Oberlin College; Priscilla Murolo, Sarah Lawrence College; Kathryn M. Olesko, Georgetown University; Kathleen A. Parrow, Black Hills

State University; Harry Ritter, Western Washington University; and Kevin Spicer, Stonehill College. Their thoughtful feedback was invaluable. I would also like to thank the thirty-seven student reviewers who offered commentary on the previous edition of this book.

At Bedford/St. Martin's, I would like to thank Chuck Christensen and Joan Feinberg, who conceived the original idea for this book. Special thanks go to my tireless and insightful editor, Kathy Retan, whose suggestions greatly improved the text and who has seen this edition through from the beginning. I would also like to thank Mary V. Dougherty, Executive Editor for History; Jane Knetzger, Director of Development for History; my production editor, Kristen Merrill; and copyeditor Lisa Flanagan.

Once again, I need to thank Susan Craig, Director of Library and Learning Resources at the Winter Park Campus of Valencia Community College, for her excellent work on Appendix B of this manual. Finally, I am particularly grateful to my husband, Martin, and my sons, Geoff and Jonathan, who have patiently supported my work on this book through five editions. You're the best.

Mary Lynn Rampolla
Trinity (Washington) University
Washington, D.C.

A Pocket Guide to Writing in History

1

Introduction:
Why Study History?

As any Harry Potter fan knows, the most boring class at Hogwarts School of Witchcraft and Wizardry is History of Magic, taught by the dead (and deadly dull) Professor Binns. The professor's droning lectures regularly send students into a stupefied trance, from which they emerge just long enough to scribble a few names or dates into their notes. Asked on one occasion about an unsolved mystery involving the school's past, Binns replies, "My subject is History of Magic. . . . I deal with facts, Miss Granger, not myths and legends."[1] Students who take their first college history class with a sense of foreboding often think that real historians, like Professor Binns, are interested only in compiling lists of names, dates, places, and "important" events that happened sometime in the past. But history is much more than this. The historian's goal is not to collect "facts" about the past, but rather to acquire insight into the ideas and realities that shaped the lives of men and women of earlier societies. Some of the beliefs and institutions of the past may seem alien to us; others are all too familiar. But in either case, when we study the people of the past, what we are really learning about is the rich diversity of human experience. The study of history is the study of the beliefs and desires, practices and institutions, of human beings.

Why should people bother studying the past in our increasingly future-oriented society? There are as many answers to this question as there are historians. First of all, a thoughtful examination of the past can tell us a great deal about how we came to be who we are. When we

---

1. J. K. Rowling, *Harry Potter and the Chamber of Secrets* (New York: Scholastic Press, 1999), 149.

study history, we are looking at the roots of modern institutions, ideas, values, and problems. Second, the effort we put into grappling with the assumptions and world views of earlier societies teaches us to see the world through different eyes. The ability to perceive and recognize the meaning of events from a perspective other than our own and to appreciate the diversity of human beliefs and cultures is of inestimable value in our increasingly complex and multicultural society. Moreover, an awareness of various perspectives encourages students of history to engage in a critical analysis of their own culture and society and to recognize and critique their own assumptions. Finally, while historians don't have crystal balls with which to predict the future, an understanding of the ways the events of the past have shaped the complex problems with which we are grappling in our own times can provide us with the kind of insight that will help us make the decisions that will shape our future.

History is a complex discipline, and historians are a diverse group. They take different approaches to their material; they interpret the events of the past in different ways; they even disagree on such basic issues as whether and to what extent historians can be objective. These debates and disagreements amongst professional historians demonstrate the passion with which they approach their subject and ensure that the study of history will always remain fresh and exciting. Regardless of their approaches, however, all historians see writing as an important tool of inquiry and communication.

In addition to introducing you to some of the basic elements of what historians do, this manual provides guidelines for writing papers in the field of history at all levels — from first year surveys to upper-division seminars. The vast majority of students enrolled in an undergraduate history course are not contemplating a career in history. Indeed, most history majors follow career paths that lead them away from the study of the past into fields like law, government, business, and international relations. Nevertheless, the techniques you will need to master to write an effective history paper — how to read critically, think analytically, argue persuasively, and write clearly — are skills that will be useful to you wherever your academic interests take you and that you will value in whatever career path you choose to follow.

1a. Historical questions

Historians come to their work with a deep curiosity about the past; to satisfy that curiosity, they ask questions. It has been suggested that historians are like detectives; it is certainly true that they ask some of the same questions: *Who? What? When? Where?* and *Why?* Some of these questions are designed to elicit "the facts" and are relatively easy to answer: *Who* was the emperor of Japan during World War II? *What* tools did eighteenth-century weavers use? *When* did the Vietnamese drive the Khmer Rouge out of Phnom Penh? *Where* did the first Continental Congress meet? Other questions, however, are less easy to answer: *Who* was Jack the Ripper? *What* were the religious beliefs of the peasants of twelfth-century Languedoc? *When* did President Nixon learn about the Watergate break-in? *Where* did the inhabitants of the original settlement at Roanoke go, and *why* did they disappear? More complex questions such as these have formed the basis of absorbing historical studies.

Historians also ask questions that help them analyze relationships between historical facts. Many of the questions historians ask, for example, reflect their interest in understanding the *context* in which the events of the past occurred. For instance, a historian interested in nineteenth-century science would not simply describe great "advances," such as Charles Darwin's publication of his theory of evolution by means of natural selection. As we know from the heated debates of our own time, science takes place within a social and cultural context, and scientific ideas can have a deep impact on politics, religion, education, and a host of other social institutions. Therefore, the historian would also ask questions about historical context: What role did political issues play in the acceptance or rejection of Darwin's theory? What other theories were current at the time, and how did they influence Darwin's thinking? Why did some theologians find his ideas threatening to religion, while others did not? What impact did larger social, political, and intellectual movements and institutions have on the study of biology in this period? In other words, historians do not examine events in isolation; rather, they try to understand the people and events of the past in terms of the unique historical context that helped to shape them.

As they explore the relationships between and among events in the past, historians also ask about the causes of events. The historical events that you will be studying and writing about can almost never be traced to a single cause, and historians are careful to avoid simplistic cause-and-effect relationships as explanations for events. For example, although the assassination of Archduke Franz Ferdinand was the event that precipitated World War I, no historian would argue that it *caused* the war. Rather, historians try to uncover the complex multiplicity of causes that grow out of the historical context in which events occurred.

Historians also ask questions about the relationship between *continuity* (events, conditions, ideas, and so on that remain the same over time) and *change*. Many of the questions historians ask reflect this interest. For example, a historian who asks, "What impact did the Black Death have on the economic and legal status of the peasants?" is interested in examining the changes brought about by the bubonic plague against the backdrop of the ongoing institution of serfdom.

Finally, while the past doesn't change, historians' interests — and the questions they ask — do. Historians, like the people they study, are part of a larger context. They are guided in their choice of subject and in their questions by their own interests and by the interests and concerns of their societies. As they ask new questions, historians look at sources in new ways. They may even discover "new" sources — sources that had always existed but had been ignored or dismissed as irrelevant. History, therefore, is a vital and dynamic discipline. We will never know all there is to know about the past because we are constantly posing new questions, and our questions, in turn, help us to see the past in new ways.

The best way to enter the world of the historian is to ask as many questions as you can about the particular historical issues you are studying. As you seek the answers to your questions, be aware of the new and more complex questions that your answers raise, and let them guide your exploration further.

1b. How this manual can help you

When you do research and writing in a history course, you become a participant in historical debate. You devise questions about historical topics, seek answers to those questions in historical sources, and come to conclusions about those topics. In the papers you write, you need to construct arguments about the conclusions you have reached and offer support for them. This manual will help you understand the process from start to finish.

Chapter 2 introduces you to working with historical sources. Chapter 3 examines the connection between critical reading and effective writing and walks you through some typical assignments given in history courses. Chapter 4 provides advice on writing history essays while Chapter 5 is devoted entirely to the research paper. Chapters 6 and 7 are designed to help you use sources effectively while avoiding plagiarism. In addition, Chapter 7 includes models for documenting the sources you are most likely to use in an undergraduate history paper. Finally, Appendix A lists additional guides to writing in history, while Appendix B provides a guide to resources students might wish to consult while doing research.

History, like the other arts and sciences, provides a window onto the ideas and beliefs, the actions and passions, of human beings. Reading and writing history entail above all an exploration of who and what we are. This manual is designed to aid you in such exploration and to help you discover the pleasures of studying history.

2
Working with Sources

As you begin to think about historical questions, you will find that your search for answers will require you to explore a wide variety of sources. You will examine written materials of all sorts. You will look at materials written in the period you are studying and read books and articles written by modern historians. You may examine maps and photographs, paintings, and pottery. Ultimately, you may discover that you need to broaden your knowledge in a wide variety of areas, for history often takes its practitioners into all manner of related fields: literary criticism, art history, and archaeology; political science, economics, and sociology. But in any case, you will need to learn how to work with the sources on which the study of history is based.

2a. Identifying historical sources

To answer their questions, historians evaluate, organize, and interpret a wide variety of sources. These sources fall into two broad categories: primary sources and secondary sources. To study history and write history papers, you will need to know how to work with both kinds of sources.

2a-1. Primary sources

Primary sources are materials produced by people or groups directly involved in the event or topic under consideration, either as participants or as witnesses. They provide the evidence upon which historians rely in order to describe and interpret the past. Some primary sources are written documents, such as letters, diaries, newspaper and magazine articles, speeches, autobiographies, treatises, census data, and marriage, birth, and death registers. In addition, historians often examine primary sources that are not written, like works of art, films, recordings, items of clothing, household objects, tools, and archaeological remains. For recent history, oral sources, such as interviews with Vietnam veterans or Holocaust survivors and other such eyewitness accounts can also be primary sources. By examining primary sources, historians gain insights into the thoughts, behaviors, and experiences of the people of the past.

When using a primary source, it is important to *examine the source itself.* Do not simply rely on another historian's analysis of the source. The purpose of writing history, after all, is to develop your *own* interpretation based on the evidence you have assembled.

2a-2. Secondary sources

Historians also use *secondary sources:* books and articles in scholarly journals that comment on and interpret primary sources. Secondary sources are extremely useful. Reading secondary sources is often the simplest and quickest way to become acquainted with what is already known about the subject you are studying. In addition, examining scholarly books and articles will inform you about the ways in which other historians have understood and interpreted events. Reading a variety of secondary sources is also the best way to become aware of the issues and interpretations that are the subject of controversy and debate among professional historians. As a student of history, you are invited to participate in these debates. Finally, secondary sources can be an important research tool. Reading them carefully can help guide you toward topics that have not yet been explored fully or about which there is controversy. Moreover, the bibliographies of secondary sources can direct you to primary sources.

As valuable as secondary sources are, you should never base a history paper on them alone, unless, of course, you are writing a historiography paper (see 3b-5). Whenever possible, you should study the events of the past in the words of people who experienced, witnessed, or participated in them.

2a-3. Primary or secondary?

The status of a source as primary or secondary depends on the focus of your research. If you are writing about the reign of the English king Richard III (1483–85) your primary sources might include edicts, chronicles composed by contemporary witnesses to the events of his reign, and letters written by foreign ambassadors to the English court. Strictly speaking, Sir Thomas More's *History of Richard III,* written in the early sixteenth century, would be a secondary source because More was not a witness to the events he describes, and he records only the evidence provided to him by others. If, however, you are writing about the depiction of Richard III in the early Tudor period, More would be a primary source.

The questions that historians pose of their sources depend in part on the nature of the sources with which they are working. Both primary and secondary sources can provide valuable information; however, they provide different kinds of information. Primary sources allow you to enter the lives and minds of the people you are studying. The documents that people wrote — sermons and wills, novels and poems — and the things that they made — music and movies, knife blades and buttons — bring you into direct contact with the world of the past. Secondary sources, on the other hand, are written by historians who can provide a broader perspective on the events of the past than the people who actually participated in them since they have more information about the context and outcome of those events, an awareness of multiple points of view, and access to more documents than any single participant. In studying nineteenth-century communes, for example, primary sources such as the diaries or letters of commune members, or the items they produced and used, can provide firsthand information about the thoughts, feelings, and daily lives of the people who lived in such communities. Primary sources would be less useful, however, in examining the larger, sociological effects of communal living. To get a better understanding of those effects, secondary sources in which historians examine several such communities over time, or study the ways in which contemporary outsiders viewed communes, might prove more useful. In your own work, you will need to use both primary and secondary sources, always keeping in mind what kinds of information each of those sources can tell you about a topic.

2b. Evaluating sources

If primary sources always told the truth, the historian's job would be much easier — and also rather boring. But sources, like witnesses in a murder case, often lie. Sometimes they lie on purpose, telling untruths to further a specific ideological, philosophical, or political agenda. Sometimes they lie by omission, leaving out bits of information that are crucial to interpreting an event. Sometimes sources mislead unintentionally because the author was not aware of all the facts, misinterpreted the facts, or was misinformed. Many are biased, either consciously or unconsciously, and contain unstated assumptions; all reflect the interests and concerns of their authors. Moreover, primary sources often conflict. As a result, one of the challenges historians face in writing a history paper is evaluating the reliability and usefulness of their sources.

Like primary sources, secondary sources may contradict each other. Several historians can examine the same set of materials and interpret them in very different ways. Similarly, historians can try to answer the same questions by looking at different kinds of evidence or by using different methods to gather, evaluate, and interpret evidence. The study of the ways in which historians have interpreted the past is called *historiography,* and knowing how to read and evaluate the work of other historians is so important that some professors may ask you to write a historiographic essay (see 3b-5). In any case, to get the most out of your reading of secondary sources, you will need to study a variety of interpretations of historical events and issues and learn how to read carefully and critically.

2b-1. Evaluating primary sources

Primary sources comprise the basic material with which historians work. Nevertheless, historians do not take the evidence provided by such sources simply at face value. Like good detectives, they evaluate the evidence, approaching their sources analytically and critically.

Since primary sources originate in the actual period under discussion, we might be inclined to trust what they say implicitly. After all, if the author is an eyewitness, why should anyone doubt his or her word? However, as any police investigator could tell you, eyewitnesses see different things and remember them in different ways. Ask two witnesses to describe what they saw, and you will readily understand why even eyewitness sources must be carefully assessed. One way in which historians evaluate primary sources is to compare them; a fact or description contained in one source is more likely to be accepted as trustworthy if other sources support or corroborate it. Another technique historians use to evaluate the reliability of a source is to identify the author's biases. We might be less inclined, for example, to believe Polydore Vergil's assertion that Richard III killed his nephews if we realize that Vergil was the official court historian for Henry VII, who killed Richard in battle and seized the English throne for himself. Historians also read their sources carefully for evidence of internal contradictions or logical inconsistencies, and they pay attention to their sources' use of language, since the adjectives and metaphors an author uses can point to hidden biases and unspoken assumptions.

In general, when you deal with written primary sources, you should always ask the following:

Tips for Writers

Questions for Evaluating Written Primary Sources

- Who is the author?
- How does the author's gender and socioeconomic class compare to the people about whom he or she is writing?
- Why did he or she write the source?
- Who was the intended audience?
- What unspoken assumptions does the text contain?
- Are there detectable biases in the source?
- When was the source composed?
- What is the historical context in which the source was written and read?
- Are there other contemporary sources to compare against this one?

When dealing with nonwritten primary sources, the following questions will be useful:

Tips for Writers

Questions for Evaluating Nonwritten Primary Sources

FOR ARTIFACTS

- When and where was the artifact made?
- Who might have used it, and what might it have been used for?
- What does the artifact tell us about the people who made and used it and the period in which it was made?

FOR ART WORKS (PAINTINGS, SCULPTURE, ETC.)

- Who is the artist and how does the work compare to his or her other works?
- When and why was the work made? Was it commissioned? If so, by whom?
- Where was the work first displayed? How did contemporaries respond to it and how do their responses compare to the ways in which it is understood now?

FOR PHOTOGRAPHS

- Who is the photographer? Why did he or she take this photograph?
- Where was the photograph first published or displayed? Did that publication or venue have a particular mission or point of view?

FOR CARTOONS

- What is the message of the cartoon? How do words and images combine to convey that message?
- In what kind of publication did it originally appear (newspaper, magazine, etc.)? Did that publication have a particular agenda or mission?
- When did the cartoon appear and how might its historical context be significant?

FOR MAPS

- What kind of map is this (topographical, political, military, etc.)?
- Where and when was the map made, and what was its intended purpose?
- Does the map contain any extraneous text or images? If so, what do they add to our understanding of the map itself?

FOR SOUND RECORDINGS

- Who made the recording and what kind of recording is it (music, speech, interview, etc.)?
- Where and when was the recording made?
- Was the recording originally intended for broadcast? If so, why was it broadcast and who was the intended audience?

EVALUATING PRIMARY SOURCES: AN EXAMPLE. In a letter written to Sheik El-Messiri in 1798, Napoleon expresses the hope that the sheik will soon establish a government in Egypt based on the principles of the Qu'ran, the sacred text of Islam. Those principles, according to Napoleon, "alone are true and capable of bringing happiness to men."[1] Should we assume, on the evidence of this letter, that Napoleon believed in the truth of Islam? A historian might ask, "Do we have any other evidence for Napoleon's attitude toward Islam? What do other primary sources tell us about Napoleon's attitude toward religions such as Catholicism, Protestantism, and Judaism? Do any other primary sources contradict the attitude toward Islam expressed in Napoleon's letter to the sheik?" In other words, "How accurately and to what extent can this source answer questions about Napoleon's religious beliefs?" In addition, historians try to understand or interpret their sources even if those sources do not offer the best or most accurate information on a certain topic. As it happens, Napoleon did not believe in Islam. This does not mean, however, that his letter to the sheik should be relegated to the dustbin. Instead, a good historian will ask, "Under what circumstances did Napoleon write this letter? Who was Sheik El-Messiri, and what was his relationship to Napoleon? What does this letter tell us about Napoleon's willingness to use religion to his political advantage?" Thus, to write about historical questions, you will need to know how to approach many different kinds of primary sources and ask appropriate questions of them.

THINKING ABOUT EDITIONS AND TRANSLATIONS. When professional historians work with primary sources, they travel to archives and libraries around the world to analyze original letters, manuscripts, photographs, and so on. When they turn to published editions of their sources, they work with these sources in their original languages. Undergraduates rarely have the opportunity or the linguistic skills to conduct this kind of research. Instead, students rely on published, translated editions of primary

---

1. Napoleon Bonaparte, "Letter to the Sheik El-Messiri," in *The Mind of Napoleon: A Selection from His Written and Spoken Words,* 4th ed., trans. and ed. J. Christopher Herold (New York: Columbia University Press, 1969), 104.

sources or, increasingly, on documents posted on the Internet, which is an excellent source for a wide variety of documents, photographs, and other primary materials.

Using modern editions of sources in translation is an excellent way to enter into the worldview of the people you are studying. Nevertheless, you should be aware that any edited text reflects, to some extent, the interests and experiences of the editor or translator. In the process of choosing excerpts, the editor of a document is making a judgment about what aspects of the source are important. For example, when Elizabeth Agassiz compiled the letters of her husband, the nineteenth-century naturalist Louis Agassiz, for publication, she eliminated passages that reveal the strong antipathy he felt toward blacks. It was only when he examined the original letters themselves that Harvard University professor Stephen Jay Gould discovered that the published letters had been expurgated.[2] The process by which the editor of a document collection selects which documents to include and which to leave out also involves interpretation. The collection, as it appears in print, reflects how the editor interprets and organizes the material and what he or she sees as significant. You should read the whole source, if possible, rather than excerpts; when you are writing a history paper, you need to know the significance of the entire document and the context of any portions of the source that you wish to discuss or quote.

The following suggestions will help you to evaluate both print and online editions of primary sources:

- Always read the preface and introduction carefully to determine the principles underlying the editor's process of selection.
- Pay careful attention to the footnotes and endnotes, which will alert you to alternate readings or translations of the material in the text.
- When using an online source, follow the links that lead you to further sources or information.
- As a rule, use the most recent edition or translation, which reflects the current state of scholarship.

---

2. Stephen Jay Gould, *The Mismeasure of Man* (New York: W. W. Norton and Co., 1981), 77.

2b-2. Evaluating secondary sources

Reading secondary sources helps us understand how other historians have interpreted the primary sources for the period being studied. Students sometimes hesitate to question the conclusions of established scholars; nevertheless, as with primary sources, it is important to read secondary sources critically and analytically, asking the same questions you ask of primary sources.

Evaluate a secondary source, as you would a primary source, by asking critical questions:

Tips for Writers

Questions for Evaluating Secondary Sources

- Who is the author? What are his or her academic credentials? (You will often find information about the author in the preface of a book; journals sometimes include authors' biographies, either on the first page of the article or in a separate section.)
- Who is the publisher? (That is, is the text published by a scholarly press, or a popular one?)
- Who is the intended audience for the text (scholars, students, general reading public, etc.)?
- When was the text written?
- Do the footnotes/endnotes and bibliography reference other important works on the same topic?
- Does the author contradict or disagree with others who have written on the subject, and if so, does he or she acknowledge and effectively address opposing arguments or interpretations?
- Does the author use primary sources as evidence to support his or her thesis? Is his or her interpretation of the primary sources persuasive?
- Is there primary source evidence that you are aware of that the author does not consider?
- Does the author build his or her argument on any unsubstantiated assumptions?

In addition, when you use a secondary source, it is especially important to do the following:

CONSIDER THE IMPLICATIONS OF THE PUBLICATION DATE. If it is important that you know the most recent theories about a historical subject, pay special attention to the publication dates of the sources you are considering. A 2000 article reviewing theories about the construction of Native American burial mounds may contain more recent ideas than a 1964 review. Do not assume, however, that newer interpretations are always better; some older works have contributed significantly to the field and may offer interpretations that are still influential. (As you become more experienced in historical research, you will be able to determine which older sources are still useful.) Moreover, older sources might offer a historical perspective on how interpretations of an issue or event have changed over time, which is particularly important if you are writing a historiographic essay.

EVALUATE THE SUPPORT THE AUTHOR PROVIDES FOR HIS OR HER THESIS. Any book or article makes an argument in support of a thesis. (For detailed information on what a thesis is and a discussion of how the thesis relates to the argument of a paper, see 4c and 4d). Once you have identified the author's thesis, you should evaluate the evidence he or she uses to support it. You may not be in a position to judge the accuracy of the evidence, although you will build expertise as you continue to read about the subject. You can, however, evaluate the way in which the author uses the evidence he or she presents. You might ask yourself whether the evidence logically supports the author's point. For example, Margaret Sanger, who founded the American Birth Control League in 1921, was also involved in the U.S. eugenics movement, which advocated, among other things, for the sterilization of individuals deemed "mentally incompetent." This, however, does not justify the conclusion that *all* early twentieth-century birth-control advocates favored eugenics. Such an assertion would be a logical fallacy known as a *hasty generalization*.

You should also ask whether the same facts could be interpreted in another way to support a different thesis. For example, G. Stanley Hall, an early twentieth-century American psychologist, amassed evidence that demonstrated a correlation between a woman's educational level and the number of children she had: Women who attended colleges and universities had fewer children than their less educated sisters. From these facts, he concluded that higher education caused sterility in women. A modern historian looking at the same evidence might conclude that education allowed women to become economically independent, freed them from the necessity of forming early marriages, and allowed them to pursue careers other than raising children.

Another consideration is whether the cause-and-effect relationships described in a source are legitimate. It may be true that event A happened before event B, but that does not necessarily mean that A caused B. For example, on July 20, 1969, Neil Armstrong became the first person to walk on the moon. The following winter was particularly harsh in the United States. We should not necessarily conclude, however, that the lunar landing caused a change in weather patterns. This would be a *post hoc* fallacy, from the Latin *post hoc, ergo propter hoc* (after this, therefore because of this).

Finally, consider how the author deals with any counterevidence. (See 4d-2 for a discussion of counterevidence.)

2b-3. Evaluating Internet sources

The Internet provides ready access to both primary and secondary sources. Editions of a wide variety of written primary sources (letters, treatises, government publications, even whole books) are available on the Web, as are cartoons, photographs, images of antique maps, and other nonwritten primary sources. If you are looking for secondary sources, historians may publish their research online in electronic journals like *The E-Journal of Portuguese History* (http://www.brown.edu/Departments/Portuguese_Brazilian_Studies/ejph/); in addition, scholarly articles are available on the Web through subscription servers such as *JSTOR: The Scholarly Journal Archive* (http://www.jstor.org/), which scans and archives a wide variety of scholarly print journals. (For a list of useful electronic sources, see Appendix B.)

Internet sites maintained by universities, museums, government agencies, and other institutions can be a gold mine for students whose access to large research libraries is limited. Making effective use of this research tool, however, requires you to anticipate and avoid the special problems that it presents. The most significant difficulty that students encounter when trying to evaluate a Web source is credibility. Although articles in scholarly journals and books from academic presses are carefully reviewed by other scholars in the field, anyone with the right software can post information on the Internet. Students should therefore be especially careful to determine the reliability of their Internet sources.

First, determine whether the source you are using is primary or secondary and ask the same questions you would use to evaluate a similar source in print. In addition, you should ask the following questions of a Web source:

Tips for Writers

Questions for Evaluating Web Sources

- Is the author's identity clear, and, if so, what are his or her academic credentials? Does the author list an academic degree? Is he or she affiliated with a college or university? Are there other websites that provide additional information about the author?

- Does the author provide evidence for his or her assertions, such as citations, bibliographies, and so on? Are the sources up to date? Are the sources for statistics included?

- Is the site affiliated with an academic institution, press, or journal? The Web address — or URL — can provide some clues to such affiliations. If ".edu" or ".gov" appears in the address, it has been posted by an educational or governmental institution, which should give you a greater degree of confidence in the material it contains.

- Is the site sponsored by a particular organization? (Look for ".org" in the URL.) Do you know anything about the interests and concerns of the person or group that publishes the site? (Check the "About" or homepage for a "mission" statement.) Does the organization seem biased?

- What is the purpose of the site? Is it designed to inform? Persuade? Sell a product?

- Does the information on the site coincide with what you have learned about the subject from other sources?

- Has the site been updated recently?

- Does the site contain useful links to other sites? Are the linked sites affiliated with reputable institutions or persons?

If you are still unsure if an Internet source is reliable, it is best to consult your professor or a reference librarian.

2b-4. Looking at historical sources: An example

In the summer of 1925, a high school teacher named John Thomas Scopes was arrested in Dayton, Tennessee, for violating the Butler Act, a state law prohibiting the teaching of Darwin's theory of evolution in public schools. Although the trial was contrived — the ACLU, which wanted to test the constitutionality of the Butler Act, had advertised that it was willing to defend anyone arrested for violating the statute, and the city fathers of Dayton, hoping to "put Dayton on the map," had asked a cooperative Scopes to play the part of defendant — it was nonetheless quickly dubbed "the trial of the century." More than three-quarters of a century later, the trial still fascinates students of history because it highlights many of the most important social issues and intellectual conflicts in American culture in the 1920s, issues that are still of vital interest today: the relationship of science and religion, the tensions between urban and rural American culture, the rights of the majority versus those of the minority, and academic freedom versus community values.

The following five primary sources (two written texts; an eyewitness account transcribed from a film; one photograph; and one cartoon) and one secondary source all illustrate the interaction between the lead attorneys in the trial: Clarence Darrow, the well-known champion of unpopular civil liberties causes, for the defense; and William Jennings Bryan, the "great commoner" and three-time Democratic presidential candidate, for the prosecution. Taken as a group, these sources illustrate some of the challenges — and pleasures — of working with historical sources.

On the seventh day of the proceedings, the defense, in an unexpected and unprecedented move, called Bryan to the stand as an "expert witness" on the Bible. Astonishingly, Bryan agreed to testify. The direct confrontation of these two larger-than-life figures provided one of the most dramatic and highly publicized moments in the trial. The following documents capture that moment.

Document 1 is a short excerpt from the trial transcripts. At this point in the proceedings, Darrow is questioning Bryan about the creation of the earth:

[DARROW:] Do you think the earth was made in six days?

[BRYAN:] Not six days of twenty-four hours.

[DARROW:] Doesn't it say so?

[BRYAN:] No, sir.

[PROSECUTING ATTORNEY A. THOMAS] STEWART: I want to interpose another objection. What is the purpose of this examination?

BRYAN: The purpose is to cast ridicule on everybody who believes in the Bible, and I am perfectly willing that the world shall know that these gentlemen have no other purpose than ridiculing every Christian who believes in the Bible.

DARROW: We have the purpose of preventing bigots and ignoramuses from controlling the education of the United States and you know it, and that is all. . . .

BRYAN: . . . I am simply trying to protect the word of God against the greatest atheist or agnostic in the United States! (Prolonged applause.) I want the papers to know I am not afraid to get on the stand in front of him and let him do his worst! I want the world to know! (Prolonged applause.)[3]

Document 2 is an excerpt from the *New York Times'* coverage of the seventh day of the trial, as it appeared in the paper on July 21, 1925:

So-called Fundamentalists of Tennessee sat under the trees of the Rhea County Court House lawn today listening to William J. Bryan defend his faith in the "literal inerrancy" of the Bible, and laughed. . . . The greatest crowd of the trial had come in anticipation of hearing Messrs. Bryan and Darrow speak, and it got more than it expected. It saw Darrow and Bryan in actual conflict — Mr. Darrow's rationalism in combat with Mr. Bryan's faith — and forgot for the moment that Bryan's faith was its own. . . . There was no pity for the helplessness of the believer come so suddenly and unexpectedly upon a moment when he could not reconcile statements of the bible with generally accepted facts. There was no pity for his admissions of ignorance of things boys and girls learn in high school. . . . These Tennesseans were enjoying a fight. That an ideal of a great man, a biblical scholar, an authority on religion, was being dispelled seemed to make no difference. They grinned with amusement and expectation. . . . And finally, when Mr. Bryan, pressed harder and harder by Mr. Darrow, confessed he did not believe everything in the Bible should be taken literally, the crowd howled.[4]

3. Jeffrey P. Moran, *The Scopes Trial: A Brief History with Documents* (Boston: Bedford/St. Martin's, 2002), 156.

4. *New York Times,* July 21, 1925, 1, in Moran, 161.

Document 3 is an account of the same event as it was remembered by an elderly Dayton native named Eloise Reed, who recalled her impressions of the famous confrontation between Darrow and Bryan in a recent documentary film.[5] Her brother had been a member of the high school football team that Scopes coached, and she had attended the trial as a twelve-year-old girl:

> The courtyard was packed. There were not enough seats to hold all of the people and they were standing around. The benches had been set up all in front of the stand so we had a seat right in front of Darrow and Bryan. And I was all set to hear the great trial going on. . . . William Jennings Bryan was sitting there with a big palm fan and a handkerchief in his hand. Darrow is in his shirtsleeves with red suspenders, which he wore. He jumped up right in front of him, took hold of his red suspenders and flipped them, and said, "Do you really believe that that whale swallowed Jonah?" . . . He just kept pushing him and pushing him. You know I wanted to get up off of that bench and go up there and kick him. It was just, I imagine people out there in the audience felt the same way to make him hush. The thing was, he was attacking the Bible. Finally the judge said to him, "Well, what do you mean. You are harassing your own witness. What you are asking him has nothing to do with the issue of this trial. We want you to put a stop to it."

Document 4 is a photograph (Figure 2.1) taken during the trial; Darrow (standing) is examining Bryan (at the left of the photograph, holding a fan).[6]

Figure 2.1 Overhead view of the Scopes Trial

5. *The Monkey Trial,* prod. and dir. Christine Lesiak, 50 minutes, A & E Entertainment, 2000, videocassette. A transcript of the film can be found online at www.pbs.org/wgbh/amex/monkeytrial/filmmore/pt.html.

6. The photograph can be found on the Web at www.law.umkc.edu/faculty/projects/trials/scopes/darrowcross.jpg.

Finally, Document 5 is a political cartoon (Figure 2.2) that appeared in the August 1, 1925, issue of *Judge*, a periodical published in New York from 1881 to 1939.[7] It depicts a stern Darrow (right) confronting a crying Bryan (left); the caption reads "There Ain't No Santy Claus!"

An observant reader would notice immediately that, while the five primary sources are all contemporary records of the Scopes trial, they represent distinctive points of view regarding Bryan's personality and the impression he made on the stand at the trial. In working with these documents, then, the historian would need to determine the perspectives that each source represents. How does each of these sources depict the demeanor and behavior of Bryan and Darrow? How are Bryan and Darrow depicted in the cartoon, and what does this imply

"THERE AIN'T NO SANTY CLAUS!"

Figure 2.2 Cartoon of Bryan and Darrow

7. The cartoon first appeared in *Judge*, August 1, 1925 (vol. 89, no. 2283), 14. It can also be found on the Web at www.law.umkc.edu/faculty/projects/Ftrials/scopes/sco_cal.htm.

about their attitudes and personalities? How do the
sources portray their confrontation at the trial? How do
Documents 1 through 4 depict the observers' response to
Bryan's testimony? Do the sources agree on any details
that would enable us to determine "what happened"?
Where do the sources disagree? What is the significance
of these contradictions, and what might account for
them? Which of the two eyewitness accounts (Documents 2 and 3) better accords with the actual transcripts
of the trial? To what extent does the *Times* reporter's status as an "outsider" give him a different perspective on
events than that of Eloise Reed, a local? Does the photograph tend to support any particular version of the
event? Was the photograph published, and, if so, where?

We might also ask questions that require not just an
analysis of the *content* of the sources, but some research
into their *background.* Why, and under what circumstances, did each of these accounts come to be recorded?
Do these circumstances affect the degree to which we
should be willing to trust them? For example, Documents
2 and 5 appeared in the *New York Times* and *Judge,* re-
spectively. What do we know about these publications?
Were they conservative or liberal? Who comprised their
general readership, and what political, social, or economic groups did they represent? Where did they stand
on the issues at the heart of the Scopes trial?

In general, then, the student should ask: What points
of view are revealed in the sources? How should my
awareness of these viewpoints affect the way I read the
texts and look at the cartoons and photographs? And, finally, are there any additional related sources to which
these should be compared?

When we turn from primary sources to a secondary
source, we can see how the work of other historians can
add to our understanding of the past. In *Summer for the
Gods,* historian Edward J. Larson offers this description
and analysis of the seventh day of the trial:

> As the inquiry departed ever further from any apparent
> connection to the Tennessee law against teaching evolu-
> tion supposedly at issue in the trial, the prosecutor ob-
> jected, "What is the purpose of this examination?"
> Darrow answered honestly. "We have the purpose of pre-
> venting bigots and ignoramuses from controlling the ed-
> ucation of the United States," he declared, "and that is
> all." That was more than enough, for it justified his efforts

to publicly debunk fundamentalist reliance on scripture as a source of knowledge about nature suitable for setting education standards. Darrow had gone to tiny Dayton, Tennessee, for precisely this purpose, with Bryan as his target. Bryan had come to defend the power of local majorities to enact a law — his law — to ban teaching about human evolution in public schools. Two hundred reporters had followed to record the epic encounter. They billed it as "the trial of the century" before it even began. . . .[8]

Later in the book, Larson returns to the same scene:

Then, with the jury still excused, [defense attorney] Hayes called Bryan as the defense's final expert on the Bible, and the Commoner again proved cooperative. Up to this point [prosecuting attorney] Stewart had masterfully confined the proceedings and, with help from a friendly judge, controlled his wily opponents. . . . Yet Stewart could not control his impetuous co-counsel and the judge seemed eager to hear the Peerless Leader defend the faith. . . . Stewart tried to end the two-hour interrogation at least a dozen times, but Bryan refused to step down. "I am simply trying to protect the word of God against the greatest atheist or agnostic in the United States," he shouted, pounding his fist in rage. "I want the papers to know I am not afraid to get on the stand in front of him and let him do his worst." The crowd cheered this outburst and every counterthrust attempted by the Commoner. Darrow received little applause but inflicted the most jabs.[9]

While primary documents are essential to the historian's work, Larson's analysis illustrates some of the ways in which secondary sources can be useful to students in their attempts to engage in historical studies. First of all, it provides a model of how historians analyze documents (in this case, the trial transcript) and use them to reconstruct a historical event. Larson's analysis also puts the primary documents into the broader context of ongoing media interest in the trial. Moreover, he provides the reader with important information about the historical background to the events of the seventh day of the trial. He tells us, for example, that a fundamentalist interpretation of the biblical story of creation was not the sole issue of concern to the participants: Bryan wanted to defend

8. Edward J. Larson, *Summer for the Gods* (New York, NY: Basic books, 1997), 6.
9. Larson, 187, 190.

the rights of local majorities to enact laws pertaining to education, while Darrow was concerned with intellectual and academic freedom. Similarly, we learn that the rest of the prosecution team did not want Bryan to take the stand and actively tried to stop the proceedings. Armed with this knowledge, the student could return to the primary sources with new questions: How did other newspapers report the events of the trial in general and the seventh day in particular? Why didn't Stewart want Bryan to testify, and why, in the face of this opposition, did Bryan insist on taking the stand? To what extent were Bryan and Darrow involved in the issues at the heart of the Scopes trial prior to the trial itself?

Reading good secondary sources, then, is not just a way to gather information. Rather, secondary sources can provide you with models for conducting your own historical research and send you back to the primary sources with fresh perspectives and new questions of your own.

These primary and secondary documents illustrate some of the complexity — and excitement — of the historian's craft. As you read and analyze primary sources, critique the interpretations of secondary sources, and develop historical interpretations of your own, you will gain essential critical skills. Moreover, you will be able to engage as an informed participant in the historical debates that still challenge and excite professional historians.

3
Reading and Writing in History: Some Typical Assignments

Most scholars would agree that reading and writing are interactive processes. Reading and thinking about a text or group of texts helps you generate new ideas for a paper. As you read, you begin to see new connections between the ideas, people, and events you are studying. You might jot down these ideas in a notebook or in the margins of the text. Reading over these notes helps you clarify the question that you want to answer in your paper and draft a preliminary outline. As you begin to write the paper, new questions arise — and this takes you back to reading, prompting you to look at the texts you have already read in new ways and find new materials that might help you answer your questions. This chapter introduces you to the process of reading actively and discusses some typical writing assignments that measure your ability to read accurately, critically, and analytically.

3a. Reading critically in history

History courses typically require a great deal of reading from a wide variety of sources, so reading is the assignment you will encounter most frequently. If your professor has assigned a textbook, you will probably be expected to read a chapter or two each week. In addition, you may be asked to read a variety of *secondary sources,* including articles from scholarly journals or books about a particular aspect of your topic. Many professors also assign *primary sources,* documents ranging from medieval chronicles to legal documents to newspaper accounts. (For a fuller discussion of primary and secondary sources, see Chapter 2.) If you are writing a research paper, you will need to find, read, and analyze a variety of sources pertaining to your topic that are not part of the reading assigned to the whole class. Since reading is such an important assignment, it is essential to give serious consideration to *how* you read.

Reading for a history course is not like reading a best-selling novel for personal enjoyment; it is not enough to skim each page once and get the gist of the story. Similarly, you should avoid the common, but not very useful, habit of reading passively, plodding through a text line by line in hopes of absorbing some of the material it contains. To do your best work in history, you will need to become an *active* reader. In contrast to passive readers, active readers are engaged in a dialogue with the text. They ask questions, make comments, and connect what they are reading to information they already know and texts they have already read. This kind of careful and critical reading is crucial both for active and intelligent participation in class discussion and for writing effective papers.

As you complete your reading assignments, you must accomplish several tasks: You need not only to *understand* the content of what you are reading but also to *evaluate* its usefulness, *analyze* its significance, and *synthesize* all of your reading into one coherent picture of the topic you are studying. The following strategies will help you do these things.

"PRE-READ" THE TEXT. Before you even begin to read, you should try to get a sense of the scope of the book or article and what it might tell you. If you are reading a book, note its subtitle, if any; examine the table of contents; check for appendices and lists of maps and/or illustrations. If you are reading an article, look for an abstract at the beginning of the text and check for section headings. For both books and articles, look at the bibliography and determine how extensive any footnotes or endnotes are. Spending a few minutes on such pre-reading tasks will help you determine how to approach your reading and consequently make it more productive. (For more on evaluating sources, see 2b.)

DETERMINE THE AUTHOR'S THESIS. Passive readers read as if everything a book or article contains is equally important; following the advice of the King of Hearts in *Alice in Wonderland*, they "begin at the beginning, go on . . . to the end, then stop," picking up bits of information somewhat haphazardly as they go. Active readers begin by identifying the author's main idea, or thesis, which enables them to read the text more effectively.

The quickest way to identify an author's thesis is to read the preface, introduction, and conclusion of a book, or the first few paragraphs of an article. It is usually in these sections that an author states his or her main points. (Looking at the last chapter of a history book is not "cheating," by the way, nor will it "spoil" the ending, unless you have been assigned a historical mystery novel, like Josephine Tey's excellent *The Daughter of Time*.)

READ WITH THE AUTHOR'S THESIS IN MIND. If you are reading a book or article about a subject that is new to you, it is tempting to get caught up in the details and try to remember all of the "facts" the author cites. However, because the historian's goal is not simply to *collect* "facts" but to *organize* and *interpret* them in a way that allows us to better understand the people and societies of the past, it is much more useful to read a book or article with an eye to understanding how an author builds an argument in support of his or her interpretation, or thesis. In order to do this, you should identify the main pieces of evidence the author cites in support of his or her conclusions. Often, the first sentence (or topic sentence) of the body paragraphs in an article or the introductory paragraphs of each chapter of a book will indicate the most important elements of an author's argument.

ASK QUESTIONS OF THE TEXT. As you read with the author's thesis in mind, you should constantly interrogate the text: What is the author's point here? Why has he or she chosen this example? Do you disagree with any points that the author makes, and if so, why?

WRITE AS YOU READ. Active readers are *physically* active, writing as they read. Writing while reading serves several functions. Taking notes helps you to remember what you have read and to find places in the text that you wanted to return to because they were important or confusing. Writing comments in the margins of the text or in a response journal will also help you remember ideas that occurred to you as you read. (Obviously, you will only want to write directly on a text if you own or have photocopied the texts you are working with. Neither the library staff nor your fellow students will appreciate written comments on library materials.) Finally, writing will help you clarify your thoughts about what you are reading and provide direction for further reading and research.

The writing that you do while reading can take many different forms; some useful suggestions include the following:

Tips for Writers

Writing as You Read

- Underline or highlight important points, including the thesis and topic sentences.
- Look up unfamiliar words in a dictionary and write their definitions in the margins of the text.
- "Talk back" to the text by writing notations in the margins. Make a note of questions you want to answer, places where you disagree with the author's argument, and cross-references to other materials you have read on the subject.
- Write summaries of your reading to ensure that you have understood the material. (See 3b-1 for advice on summaries.)
- Copy out, *in quotation marks,* any particularly striking phrases or statements that you might want to quote directly in your work, and note complete bibliographic information. (See 5d for further advice on effective note taking.)
- Keep a journal in which you can record any ideas, insights, or questions that occur to you as you read.

REVIEW WHAT YOU HAVE WRITTEN. While writing itself helps many people remember what they have read, it is particularly useful to review your notes periodically. Make sure you have answered the questions that the reading raised for you and compared the arguments of each text you are reading with the other readings for the class.

3b. Writing about reading

When students imagine the writing assignments they might receive in a history class, they usually think about short essays and research papers, which will be discussed in detail in Chapters 4 and 5. However, history students are frequently asked to write a number of types of assignments with which you may be less familiar: summaries, annotated bibliographies, reviews and critiques, and historiographic essays. Each is based on a close, critical reading of one or more texts, but each requires a slightly different approach.

3b-1. Summaries

History students are often required to read complex and difficult texts. As a result, many professors find it useful for students to write a summary, or *précis*, of a particularly challenging or complicated document, article, or section of a book.

Writing a summary requires you to condense what you have read and describe the author's ideas *in your own words;* it helps ensure that you have understood and digested the material. A summary should *not* include your reaction to or critical analysis of the text. Rather, a summary should recount the author's main point, or thesis, and the key evidence (examples, illustrations, statistics, etc.) used to support it. You should note that you will not be able to include *all* of the author's evidence; identifying the *most important* evidence is part of the challenge of writing a summary.

In writing your summary, it is *essential* that the wording and turns of phrase be entirely your own and not those of the author of the text you are summarizing. To do otherwise is plagiarism, which is no more acceptable in a summary than in any other kind of writing. (For a detailed discussion of plagiarism and how to avoid it, see Chapter 6.)

3b-2. Annotated bibliographies

When you start to study an unfamiliar topic or begin to work on a research paper, you will need to identify and evaluate the materials that will enable you to develop an understanding of the general topic and what other scholars have said about it, and form your own interpretations of the sources. In other words, you will need to generate a bibliography.

A *bibliography* is a listing of books and articles on a specific topic; it may include both primary and secondary sources. An *annotated bibliography* begins with the information included in a bibliography and then expands on it by including a brief summary of each book or article and assessing its value for the topic under discussion. An annotated bibliography, then, demonstrates your ability to gather, examine, and evaluate materials pertaining to a particular subject.

An annotated bibliography is an especially versatile and flexible assignment, so you should pay careful attention to the instructions provided by your professor. Regardless of the length or scope of the assignment, however, entries in an annotated bibliography generally follow a similar format. The entries should be arranged alphabetically by authors' last names. (See 7b-2 for complete information about how to write bibliographic entries for a variety of sources.) Following the bibliographic information, you should include an *annotation* — a short paragraph in which you describe the content of the book and its usefulness for your topic. Some elements to include in an annotation might be:

- a one-sentence description of what the book is about, including the author's thesis
- a brief description of who the author is and what his or her credentials are as an authority on the subject
- a brief description of the evidence the author uses to support his or her thesis
- a concise evaluation of the author's use of sources and the validity of his or her argument
- a brief description of the value of the book for your project

Remember that entries in an annotated bibliography should be relatively short; you will not be able to write a full analysis of a book or article, as you would in a book review or critique (see section 3b-3). Nevertheless, you will be able to indicate to the reader the overall content of the source and its value for your project.

Following are two sample annotated bibliography entries. The first is an entry for a monograph (a book focused on one specific topic); the second is for a collection of primary documents with a short historical introduction:

ANNOTATED BIBLIOGRAPHY ENTRY: MONOGRAPH

Fletcher, Richard. *The Cross and the Crescent: Christianity and Islam from Muhammad to the Reformation.* New York: Penguin/Viking, 2004.

This book examines the interactions, both positive and negative, between Christianity and Islam in the medieval and early modern periods. Fletcher, formerly a professor of medieval history at the University of York, England, argues that despite some productive interactions in the areas of trade and intellectual life, Christians and Muslims did not achieve any real measure of mutual understanding in the period under discussion. Rather, relations between the two cultures were marked by fear and hostility on the Christian side, and disdain and aloofness on the part of Muslims. Fletcher cites numerous examples to demonstrate that even in the most multicultural parts of the medieval world (Spain, Sicily, the Latin crusader states), Christians and Muslims "lived side by side, but did not blend" (p. 116). Although Fletcher's book is brief (161 pages), it is both scholarly and eminently readable, even for a non-specialist, and provides a clearly argued introduction to the subject that elucidates both Muslim and Christian viewpoints. Footnotes enable the student to pursue the sources the author used, and a narrative bibliography provides suggestions for further reading. The book also includes a useful chronology.

ANNOTATED BIBLIOGRAPHY ENTRY: DOCUMENT COLLECTION WITH HISTORICAL INTRODUCTION

Duus, Peter, ed. *The Japanese Discovery of America: A Brief History with Documents*. Boston: Bedford Books, 1997.

This book explores the relationship between Japan and the United States in the mid-nineteenth century, focusing on the dramatic differences between the two cultures and the uneasiness, confusion, and misunderstandings that arose from those differences. In a short introductory history, Duus discusses Japanese isolationism, the military and economic factors that led the United States to forcefully open relations with Japan, and the ways in which the Japanese observed and interpreted Americans and their culture. The main body of the text comprises a series of documents, including political pamphlets, autobiographies, eyewitness accounts, broadsheets, and prints. The inclusion of both Japanese and American views of Japan invites a comparison of mutual misunderstandings.

3b-3. Book reviews and critiques

In order to demonstrate your ability to read a text critically and analytically, you may be asked to review a book or critique an article. Students sometimes feel unqualified to complete such an assignment; after all, the author of the text is a professional historian. However, even if you cannot write from the same level of experience and knowledge as the author, you *can* write an effective review if you understand what the assignment requires.

A review or a critique of a text begins with careful, active, and critical reading. (See section 3a for advice on reading critically.) You should approach the text you are going to critique as an active reader, keeping the author's thesis in mind, noting the evidence he or she uses to support that thesis, asking the critical questions for evaluating sources outlined in Chapter 2, and noting your reactions and responses to the text as you go. Your review then grows out of this active reading.

A review or critique is not the same thing as a book report, which simply summarizes the content of a book. Nor does a critique merely report your reaction (i.e., "This book was boring" or "I liked this article.") Rather, when writing a review or critique, you not only report on the content of the text and your response to it but also assess its strengths and weaknesses. So, for example, it is not enough to say "This book is not very good"; you need to explain and/or justify your reaction through an analysis of the text. Did you find the book unconvincing because the author did not supply enough evidence to support his or her assertions? Is the logic faulty? Or did you disagree with the book's underlying assumption? Finally, you should note that *critical* does not mean *negative*. If a book is well written and presents an original thesis supported by convincing evidence, say so. A good book review does not have to be negative; it *does* have to be fair and analytical. (Incidently, when you are writing your review, it is unnecessary to preface statements with "I think" or "in my opinion" since readers assume that as a reviewer you are expressing your own opinions.)

Though there is no one correct way to structure a review, the following is a possible approach:

- Summarize the book or article and relate the author's main point, or thesis. Make sure you briefly identify the author and note his or her credentials.
- Describe the author's viewpoint and purpose for writing; note any aspects of the author's background that are important for understanding the text.

- Note the most important evidence the author presents to support his or her thesis.
- Evaluate the author's use of evidence and describe how he or she deals with counterevidence. (See 4d-2 for a discussion of counterevidence.) Is the argument convincing?
- Compare this text with other books or articles you have read on the same subject.
- Conclude with a final evaluation of the book or article. You might discuss who would find it useful and why.

NOTE: While many of the elements of a review or critique are the same as those found in an annotated bibliography entry, your analysis of the text should be much fuller and more detailed.

3b-4. Film reviews

You may be surprised to find a discussion of film reviews in a chapter called "Reading and Writing in History." However, a discussion of film in this context is appropriate for two reasons. First, while historians primarily rely on written texts, film and other visual texts have become increasingly important historical sources. Second, watching a film, like reading a book, should not be a passive exercise. If you use film as a historical source, you will need to approach or "read" a film with the same critical and analytical skills that you would apply to a written text.

Just as there are different kinds of written texts, so too are there different kinds of films. The most common types of films historians use are documentaries and feature films. Identifying which type of film you are dealing with is the essential first step in writing a film review.

Documentaries

Documentaries are films that use primary sources (like photographs, paintings, and documents) and commentaries on those sources by various authorities (such as historians, biographers, and eyewitnesses) to construct a narrative of a historical figure or event. For this reason, documentaries should be considered secondary sources. Ken Burns's series *The Civil War*, which uses primary sources such as documents and photographs as well as commentary from historians, is a good example of this type of film.

Documentaries about events of the twentieth and twenty-first centuries are able to make use of a unique primary source: *footage.* Footage is a direct film or videotape recording of an event. Footage can be produced by professionals, such as television news videographers, or by amateurs, like Abraham Zapruder's 8mm film of the assassination of John F. Kennedy. Footage is a primary source since it records events as they happen.

A documentary filmmaker's use of primary sources such as footage must be viewed critically. Filmmakers, like writers, choose what to record. (Sometimes luck plays a part in the images they capture; filmmaker Jules Naudet was working on a documentary about the New York City Firefighting Academy when he filmed the highjacked plane hitting Tower 1 of the World Trade Center on September 11, 2001.) Usually, however, they are filming with a particular purpose, and sometimes with a particular audience in mind. Moreover, footage that makes its way to a news broadcast has been cut and edited. In evaluating a documentary that uses footage, it is useful to know why and by whom the original footage was shot and whether and for what purposes it has been edited.

Feature films

Feature films are films designed primarily as entertainment. They sometimes feature famous actors and always aim at box-office success. Historical rigor is not usually their primary concern, so we should not be surprised to find that such films vary dramatically in the accuracy with which they depict the period, events, and historical figures they ostensibly portray. At one end of the spectrum are films like *The Return of Martin Guerre,* which is based on a true story about a peasant who abandoned his family and the impostor who "returned" and successfully took his place. The director, Daniel Vigne, consulted historical documents, attempted faithfully to recreate the material culture of the period, and made extensive use of the expertise of historian Natalie Zemon Davis as a consultant. Consequently, this film might be considered a secondary source for our understanding of French peasant life in seventeenth-century France. In contrast, in his 1916 film *Joan the Woman,* legendary director Cecil B.

DeMille took serious liberties with the historical accounts of Joan of Arc, inventing a love interest for her and linking her story with the English efforts against the Germans in France during World War I. DeMille's film has virtually no value as a secondary source for the history of Joan of Arc, but it is a valuable primary source for understanding American attitudes towards the First World War and the role of filmmakers in encouraging the United States to join the conflict. This points to an important consideration: *all* feature films can be viewed as primary sources for the cultural and social history of the period in which they were made.

Because of the growing importance of film of all sorts, writing a film review is an increasingly common assignment. The suggestions provided in section 3b-3 for writing a book review also apply to a film review. In addition, you should do the following:

- Determine whether the film is a documentary or a feature film. Who is the intended audience, and for what reason was the film made?
- If the film is a documentary, note the academic credentials of the experts who provide the commentary. If it is a feature film, determine whether the filmmaker made use of professional historians as consultants.
- For documentaries and feature films, analyze the interests and concerns of the producer, director, and screenwriter. Note any other films they have produced, directed, or written that might help the viewer understand their interests and biases. In this context, it is useful to determine whether the people most responsible for the film have provided interviews or written commentary that might shed light on their work.
- Think about how the visual images presented in the film enhance our understanding of the subject and the period. Do the costumes and sets accurately portray the historical reality of the period? Does the film help us understand the material culture of the period?
- Analyze the cinematic techniques that are used to convey the story. Is the film shot in black and white or in color? How does the filmmaker use lighting to convey a mood or to make a symbolic point? How

is one set of images juxtaposed with another to create an impression? What kinds of camera angles are
used, and why?

- Analyze how the filmmaker uses sound. What kind
  of music is used in the soundtrack? Was it composed specifically for the film, or are classical or
  popular pieces used?
- Discuss the ways in which the filmmaker shapes
  the narrative. From what point of view is the story
  told? Does the film employ flashbacks or narrative
  voice-overs?
- If the film is based on a play or a specific text, compare the film with the original source. Are there any
  themes or concepts portrayed more effectively in
  the film than in the text? On the other hand, are
  there elements of the source that are eliminated or
  distorted in the film?
- Compare the film with other films, books, and articles on the same subject.

3b-5. Historiographic essays

As noted in Chapter 1, historians frequently disagree
about how to interpret the events they study. For example, some historians have interpreted the Magna
Carta, a charter signed by King John of England in 1215,
as a revolutionary declaration of fundamental individual
freedoms; others have seen it as a conservative restate-
ment of feudal privilege. These differences in interpretation reflect the varying approaches that historians take to
their subject. For example, individual historians might be
primarily interested in social, cultural, political, economic, legal, or intellectual history. They might approach
their work from a Marxist, Freudian, feminist, or post-
modernist point of view. Such orientations and affiliations affect the ways in which a historian explores and
interprets the past; thus, historians interested in the same
historical event might examine different sets of sources to
answer the same question. For example, in studying the
causes of the French Revolution, Marxist historians might
focus on economic and class issues, while intellectual historians might concentrate on the impact of the writings
of the philosophes (a group of French Enlightenment
writers) on political thought and practice. Moreover,
since the historian's work is embedded in a particular social and cultural context, historical interpretations and

methodologies change over time. For example, the growth of the civil rights and feminist movements in the 1960s led to a greater interest in African American and women's history. In order to make students aware of a variety of interpretations and allow them to enter the exciting world of historical discussion and debate, some instructors ask their students to write historiographic essays.

A *historiographic essay* is one in which you, acting as a historian, study the approaches to a topic that other historians have taken. When you write a historiographic essay, you identify, compare, and evaluate the viewpoints of two or more historians writing on the same subject. Such an essay can take several forms. You might be asked, for example, to study the work of historians who lived during or near the time in which a particular event happened — for example, to explore the ways in which contemporary Chinese historians wrote about the Boxer Rebellion. A different kind of historiographic essay might require that you look at the ways in which historians have treated the same topic over time. For example, to examine how historians have treated Thomas Jefferson, you might begin with two pre–Civil War biographies — Matthew L. Davis's *Memoirs of Aaron Burr* (1836–37), which provides a scathing critique of Jefferson, and Henry S. Randall's contrastingly positive *Life of Jefferson* (1858) — and end with the most recent studies of Jefferson. Yet another such assignment might ask you to compare the views of historians from several historical schools on the same event. You might, for example, be asked to compare Whig and Progressive interpretations of the American Revolution or Marxist and feminist views of the French Revolution. Historiographic essays may be short or quite lengthy. In any case, a historiographic essay focuses attention not on a historical event itself but rather on how historians have interpreted that event.

A historiographic essay combines some of the features of a book review with those of a short essay or research paper. You should begin by reading critically the texts containing historians' interpretations, keeping in mind the questions you would need to answer if you were going to write book reviews about them (see 3b-3). You should not, however, treat the historiographic essay as two or three book reviews glued together. Rather, you should synthesize your material and construct an argument in support of a thesis. The following thesis is from a student's essay on historians' interpretations of the colonial period of African history:

> Historians have held dramatically different views about the importance of European colonial rule in Africa: Marxist historians, along with others who focus on economic issues, have tended to see the colonial period as an important turning point, while cultural historians have maintained that the impact of the West on the ancient cultural traditions of Africa was superficial.

In the rest of the paper, the student supports the thesis as he or she would do in any other history paper. (For a fuller discussion of formulating and supporting a thesis, see 4c and 4d.)

3c. Taking history exams

History exams reflect your ability to synthesize all of the materials you have examined over the course of a semester into a coherent picture of the period you are studying. If you have been attending classes and reading actively and critically throughout the semester, the final exam should not be an occasion for panic but rather a chance to demonstrate your understanding of the people, events, and institutions you have been studying.

History exams can follow many different formats. One typical component of a history exam that allows the professor to evaluate the students' basic mastery of the material is a series of identification questions that ask students to briefly describe and note the significance of important persons, places, or events. Many instructors also test their students' ability to synthesize the material they have been studying throughout the semester by asking them to write short essays that discuss a particular historical question or issue in some detail. Since history exams can vary widely in format, it is important to pay careful attention to your professor's specific instructions. The following general advice, which includes strategies for answering identification questions and composing short essays, can help you prepare for any history exam.

3c-1. Preparing for an exam

The best preparation for an exam does not begin the day, or even the week, before the exam but takes place throughout the semester. Careful reading of the texts and periodic review of your notes will ensure that you have a firm grasp of the material come exam time.

Throughout the semester, you should do the following:

ATTEND CLASS REGULARLY AND TAKE GOOD NOTES. It is not necessary to write down *everything* your professor says. When taking notes, you should listen for the *main points* and note the evidence given to support those points. (You will discover that your professor's lectures usually follow the same format as a good essay.) Follow the same suggestions for a discussion class; your classmates will often make important points about the material you are studying.

REVIEW YOUR NOTES REGULARLY, PREFERABLY AFTER EACH CLASS. If you review your notes while the class is fresh in your mind, it will be easier for you to notice places where the notes are unclear. Mark these places, and clarify confusing points as soon as possible, either by researching the issue yourself or by asking your professor.

KEEP A LIST OF IMPORTANT IDEAS, PEOPLE, AND EVENTS. As you read your texts and review your class notes, it is useful to make a list of significant persons, places, events, and concepts along with a brief description of why they are important. Look up the definitions of terms with which you are unfamiliar. This will not only ensure that you understand the key ideas in the material you are studying, but will also be particularly useful if your exam for the course includes an identification section. How do you know which items to include on this list? Some will be obvious; if you are taking a course called The Age of Dictators, it would be a good thing to be able to identify Hitler, Mussolini, and Stalin. In cases in which the importance of a person or an idea is not so obvious, look for other clues: words that are italicized in your texts; concepts that recur in several of your readings; and terms, events, or people that your professor has highlighted for you or written on the board.

REFER TO YOUR SYLLABUS THROUGHOUT THE SEMESTER. Many instructors provide detailed syllabi that state the themes for each section of the course. Use the syllabus as a guide for your own studying and thinking about the course material.

TAKE CAREFUL NOTES ON THE READING. Read with a notebook or computer at hand, and take notes as you read. Keep in mind that simply copying long sections from your texts is not very useful in ensuring that you have understood the material. It will be much more useful for you to take notes in the form of summaries. (See 3b-1 for a fuller discussion.)

KEEP AN ACADEMIC JOURNAL. Some professors require students to keep academic journals, but even if this is not the case for your class, you should consider doing so. In your journal, record important points about the material you are reading, any questions you want to answer or issues you would like to raise, important ideas suggested by class discussions, and so on. Use the journal to track your growing knowledge of the material you are studying.

The week before the exam, you should do the following:

REVIEW YOUR NOTES, SYLLABUS, AND TEXTS. Identify the most important themes and issues of the course, and assemble the evidence that clarifies those themes.

ANTICIPATE QUESTIONS. Imagine that you are the professor faced with the task of creating the exam for this course. What questions would you ask? Framing your own exam questions and answering them can be a useful way of organizing your thoughts.

3c-2. Answering identification questions

Professors often use identification questions as a way of testing your basic understanding of the material covered in the course. You may be asked to identify people, places, or events, or to define important concepts. If you have kept a running list of significant individuals, events, and terms, you probably will not be surprised by any of the items in the identification section of your test.

When answering identification questions, it is important to *read the directions carefully*. Students tend to make one of two mistakes in answering identification questions. On the one hand, they may produce answers that are too detailed. The response to an identification question should not be a full-blown, four-page essay. So, how much should you write? Often, your professor will tell you how long your response should be; you might, for example, be asked to answer in one sentence or to write a three- to four-sentence paragraph. The number of points an identification answer is worth also provides a clue to how much time you should spend writing your response. If your exam includes an essay worth 50 points, and ten identifications worth 5 points each, you obviously should not spend thirty minutes on one identification.

The second mistake is to write too little. Again, if each identification is worth 5 points, identifying Anne Boleyn as "an English queen" is clearly not enough; dozens of people can be identified as English queens. Your answer should be specific enough to identify the individual person, event, or concept. Thus, a more successful response to an identification question on Anne Boleyn would include the information that she was the second wife of Henry VIII and the mother of Queen Elizabeth I. Moreover, identification questions may ask you to go one step further by noting the significance of the person, event, or concept. Sometimes, this expectation is spelled out in the directions; you are instructed to "identify and *explain the significance of* the following." At other times, the suggested length of your answer provides the clue; if you are asked to write three to four sentences, you will need to provide more than a minimal identification. In this instance, thinking about why your professor has asked you to identify particular persons, events, or concepts will help you to formulate your answer.

3c-3. Taking an essay exam

The essays you write for an exam will necessarily be shorter than the papers you write for your course, but they should follow the same basic format. In other words, an exam essay should begin with a thesis stated clearly in the first paragraph, followed by several paragraphs in which you provide evidence supporting your thesis, and end with a conclusion. (For detailed advice on writing a history essay, see Chapter 4). The difficulty, of course, is that you will be writing *this* essay under pressure, in a limited period of time, and without the opportunity to check the accuracy of your data.

Here are some suggestions for writing a successful essay on a history exam.

PREPARING TO WRITE. *Do not begin to write right away.* This is probably the biggest mistake that students make in essay exams. Before you write, do the following:

- Read the exam carefully. Make sure you understand what each question is really asking. You will not gain points by scribbling down everything you know about the development of Chinese politics from the tenth through the fifteenth century when the question asks you to discuss the impact of the Mongol invasion in 1260.
- If you are offered a choice, make sure you answer the question you can answer best. This may not always be the one you are drawn to first. One great insight about the significance of the Treaty of Waitangi will not be enough to write a good essay about Maori-British relations in nineteenth-century New Zealand. Be sure that you can cite several pieces of evidence in support of your thesis.
- Take the time to organize your thoughts. Jot down a quick outline for your essay, stating the thesis and listing the evidence you will provide to support that thesis.

WRITING THE ESSAY. Once you are ready to write, your essay should follow the same format as any other history essay:

- Begin by stating your thesis. *Do not* waste time restating the question: Your professor knows what he or she asked.
- Cite the evidence that supports your thesis. If you are aware of any counterevidence, make sure you discuss it. (See 4d-2 for a discussion of counterevidence and how to deal with it.)
- Be sure you stick to the point. Do not go off on interesting tangents that are irrelevant to the question. Referring frequently to your outline will help keep you on track.
- Tie your essay together by stating your conclusions.

4
Following Conventions of Writing in History

Each academic discipline has its own practices, or conventions, that people writing in the discipline follow when engaged in a scholarly dialogue. Following the conventions for writing in history will make it easier for you to participate in an academic conversation in your field. Moreover, many historians are excellent stylists. Your instructor will pay attention to your writing, so your attempts to learn and follow the conventions of the discipline will be noticed — and worth the effort.

History students are most often asked to write two types of papers: short essays and research papers. For either of these assignments, you should follow a similar process. First, you must analyze the assignment, identifying what it requires of you. Then, as you examine the sources, you will need to keep in mind some of the special conventions governing historical research, such as understanding historical events and people within their own context and avoiding anachronism. As you develop a piece of writing, you will need to move from the assigned topic to a thesis, build an argument based on evidence in support of that thesis, and organize your paper effectively. Finally, you will need to revise and edit your paper, paying special attention to grammar, word choice, and usage.

This chapter provides advice on all aspects of writing a short essay. Unlike most research papers, essays are relatively brief (ranging from as little as 3–4 pages up to

8–10 pages), and the topic and texts are usually assigned. Research papers, which build on the techniques required for writing an effective essay, are considered in Chapter 5.

4a. Analyzing an assignment

The first thing you will need to do when faced with the task of writing a short essay in history is to analyze the assignment, making sure that you identify and understand *all* of its parts—that you are aware of what, exactly, the assignment is asking you to do. This assignment, for example, is from a course on the history of Christian-Muslim relations:

> Compare the ways in which Fulcher of Chartres (a medieval Christian historian) and Ibn al-Athir (a medieval Muslim historian) explain the Christian success at the siege of Antioch during the First Crusade.

In approaching this assignment, you should first note that you will need to understand what *both* Fulcher of Chartres and Ibn al-Athir thought about the siege of Antioch and give *approximately equal weight* to each in your discussion; it would not be sufficient to write a paper about Fulcher using a few references to Ibn al-Athir for comparison. Second, because the assignment asks for a comparison, you will need to discuss both how the two accounts are similar and how they differ; in other words, an essay that asks you to compare two things also, by implication, asks you to consider contrasts.

Once you have understood the parameters of the assignment, you should assess the *significance* of the issue you are examining. For the assignment given above, for example, your paper should not take the form of two mini-papers — one on Fulcher and one on Ibn al-Athir — glued together, since this does not constitute a thoughtful comparison. Nor should you present a laundry list of similarities and differences. Keep in mind that merely reporting the content of a text or texts does not constitute a history essay; underlying every essay assignment in history are the questions "So what?" and "Why is this important?" In the sample assignment, the instructor's expectation is that the student will not only identify the ways in which the two authors are similar and different but will analyze the *meaning* of those similarities and differences and explain why they are significant. You might discover, for example, that Fulcher and Ibn al-Athir agree that the gates to Antioch were opened for the Christian army by a Muslim cuirass-maker. However, they differ in their interpretation of this event. Ibn al-Athir describes the event in purely secular terms, noting that the traitor succumbed to bribery, while Fulcher maintains that his actions were the result of three visions, thus demonstrating God's direct involvement in human affairs. What can we learn from this comparison of the authors' assumptions about God and history?

You should also think about the historical issue underlying the assignment. In this essay assignment, the student is asked to compare the views of a medieval Christian writer with those of a medieval Muslim. One purpose of this assignment might be to encourage the student to think about the degree to which medieval authors from different religious cultures shared a common set of beliefs about the world: What ideas do they share, and how and why do their worldviews differ?

Finally, you should be careful to write about the topic that has actually been assigned. In reading Fulcher and Ibn al-Athir, for example, you may discover that both authors discuss the importance of Jerusalem in their respective religions. Although this is an interesting and important topic, it is not the subject of the assignment.

4b. Thinking like a historian

Before you begin to write your essay, you need to become familiar with a number of conventions that historians have established to govern their relationship with their subject; in other words, you need to learn how to think like a historian. Learning these conventions will enable you to be an active participant in historical conversations.

RESPECT YOUR SUBJECT. When you write a history paper, you are forming a relationship of sorts with real people and events whose integrity must be respected. The people who lived in the past were not necessarily more ignorant or cruel (or, conversely, more innocent or moral) than we are. It is condescending, for example, to suggest that any intelligent or insightful person was "ahead of his or her time" (suggesting, of course, that he or she thought the same way we do).

DO NOT GENERALIZE. Remember that groups are formed of individuals. Do not assume that everyone who lived in the past believed the same things or behaved the same way. Avoid broad generalizations, such as "the medieval period was an Age of Faith" or "pre-modern people were not emotionally attached to their children." At best, such statements are clichés. More often than not, they are also wrong.

AVOID ANACHRONISM. An anachronistic statement is one in which an idea, event, person, or thing is represented in a way that is not consistent with its proper historical time or context. For example, "Despite the fact that bubonic plague can be controlled with antibiotics, medieval physicians treated their patients with ineffective folk remedies." This sentence includes two anachronisms. First, although antibiotics are effective against bubonic plague, they had not yet been discovered in the fourteenth century; it is anachronistic to mention them in a discussion of the Middle Ages. Second, it is anachronistic to judge medieval medicine by modern standards. A more effective discussion of the medieval response to the bubonic plague would focus on fourteenth-century knowledge about health and disease, theories of contagion, and sanitation practices. In short, you should not import the values, beliefs, and practices of the present into the past. Try to understand the people and events of the past in their own contexts.

BE AWARE OF YOUR OWN BIASES. We naturally choose to write about subjects that interest us. Historians should not, however, let their own concerns and biases direct the way they interpret the past. A student of early modern Europe, for example, might be dismayed by the legal, social, and economic limitations placed on women in that period. Reproaching sixteenth-century men for being "selfish and chauvinistic" might forcefully express such a student's sense of indignation about what appears to modern eyes as unjust, but it is not a useful approach for the historian, who tries to understand the viewpoints of people in the past in the social context of the period under study.

4c. Moving from topic to thesis

Your *topic* is the subject you have been assigned to write about (the Salem witchcraft trials, the Lewis and Clark expedition, the rise of the Nazi party). If you merely collect bits of information about your topic, however, you will not have written an effective history paper. A history paper, like many other kinds of academic writing, usually takes the form of an argument in support of a *thesis* — the conclusion you have reached about your topic after a careful analysis of the sources.

A thesis is *not* a description of your paper topic, a question, a statement of fact, or a statement of opinion, although it is sometimes confused with all of these things. Consider the following essay assignment: "Discuss the role of nonviolent resistance in the Indian independence movement." Although your reader should not have to guess what your paper is about, the thesis must do more than announce your subject or the purpose for which you are writing. "This paper is about the role of nonviolent resistance in the Indian independence movement" is not a thesis statement; nor is "The purpose of this paper is to describe the methods Mohandas Gandhi used to gain Indian independence from Great Britain." These sentences merely restate the assigned topic. Similarly, although historians always ask questions as they read (see 3a for advice on active reading), and a thesis statement arises from the historian's attempt to answer a question, a question is not, in itself, a thesis. "Why were Mohandas Gandhi's methods successful in the movement to achieve Indian independence from Great Britain?" is a valid historical question, but it is not a thesis statement. Moreover, while historians deal in factual information about the past, a "fact," however interesting, is simply a piece of data. The statement "Mohandas Gandhi led the movement by which India achieved independence from Britain" is not a thesis. Finally, although a thesis statement must reflect what you have concluded, it cannot be a simple statement of belief or preference. The assertion "Mohandas Gandhi is my favorite political leader of the twentieth century" does not constitute a thesis.

A thesis is a statement that reflects what you have concluded about the topic of your paper, based on a critical analysis and interpretation of the source materials you have examined. The following sentence *is* an acceptable thesis: "From the moment that Mohandas Gandhi decided to respond to force with acts of civil disobedience, British rule of India was doomed; his indictment of British colonial policy in the court of public opinion did far more damage to the British military than any weapon could." You should note two things about this statement. First, the thesis is an answer to the question posed above: "Why were Mohandas Gandhi's methods successful in the movement to achieve Indian independence from Great Britain?" A thesis usually arises from the questions you pose of the text or texts as you engage in active reading. Second, a thesis is always an arguable point, a conclusion with which a thoughtful reader might disagree. It is the writer's job, in the body of a paper, to provide an argument based on evidence that will convince the reader that his or her thesis is a valid one. The thesis, then, is the heart of your paper. It presents what you have concluded about the topic under discussion, and provides the focal point for the rest of the essay.

To ensure that your thesis really *is* a thesis, keep the following tips in mind:

Tips for Writers

Formulating an Effective Thesis Statement

If . . .	Then . . .
Your "thesis" statement does no more than repeat the topic you are writing about	It is *not* a thesis.
Your "thesis" statement poses a question without proposing an answer	It is *not* a thesis.
Your "thesis" statement merely articulates a fact or series of facts	It is *not* a thesis.
Your "thesis" statement simply reflects a personal belief or preference	It is *not* a thesis.
Your "thesis" statement: proposes an answer to a question you have posed as a result of your reading AND	

Formulating an Effective Thesis Statement, continued	
If . . .	**Then . . .**
asserts a conclusion with which a reader might disagree, and which can be supported by evidence from the sources	It *is* an effective thesis.

4d. Constructing an argument

One reason that students often find it difficult to develop a thesis statement is that they are hesitant to come to independent conclusions about the meaning and significance of the materials with which they are working; after all, what if their interpretation is wrong? It often seems safer just to reiterate the topic, or ask a question, or state a fact with which no one could argue. But, as noted in the previous section, to write an effective history paper you must be willing to reach a conclusion about your subject that could be challenged or debated by an intelligent reader. While this may seem intimidating, you should keep in mind that historical issues are seldom clear-cut and that professional historians, working from the same sources, often disagree with each other or form very different interpretations. It is unlikely that there is one "correct" point of view concerning the topic you have been assigned or one "correct" interpretation of the sources you are examining. You do not need to convince your readers that your thesis or argument represents the *only* possible interpretation of the evidence. You do, however, need to convince them that your interpretation is a *valid* one. You will be able to do this only if you have provided concrete evidence from reliable sources in support of your argument, and have responded honestly to opposing positions.

4d-1. Supporting your thesis

To support your argument, you must offer evidence from your sources. Imagine that you have been given the following assignment in a course on the history of science: "Analyze the role played by experiment and observation in William Harvey's *On the Motion of the Heart and Blood*." A student writing an essay on this topic would have noticed that Harvey describes his experimental method and his observations in great detail. She would also have noticed, however, that Harvey drew inspiration from the analogy he saw between the sun as the center of the solar system and the heart as the center of the body, and that this analogy led him to consider whether the blood, like the planets, might move about the body in a circular motion. Her thesis will depend on the conclusion she has reached, after careful and active reading of the text, about which of these elements was more significant in his discovery of circulation. If she concludes that experimentation and observation were more important in Harvey's thinking, her thesis statement might look like this:

> Although Harvey sometimes used analogies and symbols in his discussion of the movement of the heart and the blood, it was his careful observations, his elegantly designed experiments, and his meticulous measurements that led him to discover circulation.

If, on the other hand, she concluded that Harvey's philosophical commitments were more significant, she might write the following:

> Harvey's commitment to observation and experiment mark him as one of the fathers of the modern scientific method; however, a careful reading of *On the Motion of the Heart and Blood* suggests that the idea of circulation did not arise simply from the scientific elements of his thinking, but were inspired by his immersion in neo-Platonic philosophy.

Note the writer of this essay could come to *either* of these conclusions after a careful examination of the text; neither is "right" or "wrong." What is essential is that the student support her thesis by constructing an argument with evidence taken from the text itself. It is *not* enough simply to make an assertion and expect readers to agree. In the first instance, she would support her thesis by pointing to examples of experiments Harvey designed and carried out. She might also note his emphasis on quantification, and the care with which he described experiments that could be replicated. In the second instance, she might note the number of times Harvey compares the heart to the sun (thus providing an analogy for "circulation"). She might also note that Harvey was unable to actually observe circulation, since capillaries are too small to be seen with the microscopes available at the time, and that his belief in circulation therefore required an intuitive leap that could not have been drawn solely from observation or experiment.

4d-2. Responding to counterevidence and anticipating opposing viewpoints

Acknowledging counterevidence — source data that does not support your argument — will not weaken your paper. On the contrary, if you address counterevidence effectively, you strengthen your argument by showing why it is legitimate despite information that seems to contradict it. If, for example, the student writing about Harvey wanted to argue for the primacy of experiment and observation in his work, she would need to show that these elements were more significant than his interest in philosophical speculation. If she wanted to argue that his philosophy was more important, she would have to demonstrate that it was his keen interest in the ways in which some philosophers interpreted the centrality of the sun in the universe as a metaphor that allowed him to interpret what he observed about the movement of the blood and the heart in creative new ways. In either case, her argument would need to be based on a consideration of the evidence and counterevidence contained in the relevant source or sources, not merely on her own gut feelings.

Similarly, if you are writing an essay in which you are examining secondary sources, you should demonstrate that you are aware of the work of historians whose interpretations differ from your own; never simply ignore an argument that doesn't support your interpretation. It is perfectly legitimate to disagree with others' interpretations; this is, after all, one of the purposes of writing a book review or a historiographic essay. (See sections 3b-3 and 3b-5.) In disagreeing, however, it is important to treat opposing viewpoints with respect; you should never resort to name-calling, oversimplifying, or otherwise distorting opposing points of view. Your essay will be stronger, not weaker, if you understand opposing arguments and respond to them fairly.

A good argument, then, does not ignore evidence or arguments that seem to contradict or weaken the thesis. If you discover information that does not support your thesis, do not suppress it. It is important to acknowledge *all* of your data. Try to explain to readers why your interpretation is valid, despite the existence of counterevidence or alternative arguments, but do not imply that your interpretation is stronger than it is by eliminating data or falsifying information. Rather, a successful paper would respond to counterevidence and differing interpretations by addressing them directly and explaining why, in your view, they do not negate your thesis.

4e. Organizing your paper

Even after analyzing an assignment, reading the sources carefully with a historian's eyes, developing a thesis, and finding evidence in the sources that supports your thesis, you may still find it difficult to organize your ideas into an effective paper. History papers, like other academic writing, include an introduction, a body, and a conclusion. This section examines the specific elements that your history instructor will expect to find in each of these parts of your paper.

4e-1. Drafting an introduction

The introductory paragraph of your paper is in many ways the most important one and, therefore, the most difficult to write. In your introduction, you must (1) let your readers know what your paper is about, (2) put the topic of your paper into context, and (3) state your thesis. You must also attract your readers' attention and interest. The opening paragraph, then, has to frame the rest of the paper and make readers want to continue reading.

There is no magic formula for writing an effective first paragraph. You should, however, keep the following conventions in mind.

DO NOT OPEN WITH A GLOBAL STATEMENT. Unsure of how to start, many students begin their papers with phrases like "Throughout history" or "From the beginning of time" or "People have always wondered about . . . " You should avoid broad generalizations like these. First, you cannot prove that they are true: How do you know what people have always thought or done? Second, these statements are so broad that they are virtually meaningless; they offer no specific points or details to interest readers. Finally, such statements are so general that they give readers no clue about the subject of your paper. In general, it is much more effective to begin with material that is specific to your topic.

The following opening sentence comes from the paper on William Harvey's *On the Motion of the Heart and Blood:*

INEFFECTIVE

From ancient times, people have always been interested in the human body and how it works.

Although, strictly speaking, there is nothing wrong with this sentence, it is not a particularly effective opening. For one thing, it is such a general statement that readers will be inclined to ask, "So what?" In addition, it gives readers no indication of what the paper is about. Will the essay examine ancient Greek medical theory? Chinese acupuncture? Sex education in twentieth-century American schools?

In revising the sentence, the student eliminated the general statement altogether and began instead with a description of the intellectual context of Harvey's work:

EFFECTIVE

For the scholars and physicians of seventeenth-century Europe, observation and experimentation began to replace authoritative texts as the most important source of information about human anatomy and physiology.

From this short sentence, readers learn four things about the subject of the paper: the time frame of the discussion (the seventeenth century), the place (Europe), the people involved (scholars and physicians), and the topic (the importance of experiment and observation in the biological sciences). Readers' curiosity is also piqued by the questions implied in the opening statement: Why did experimentation begin to replace authoritative texts? Was this change a subject of controversy? Who was involved? How did this change in method affect the science of biology and the practice of medicine? In other words, this opening sentence makes readers want to continue reading; they want to know the author's thesis.

INCLUDE YOUR THESIS IN THE FIRST PARAGRAPH. If your opening sentence has been effective, it will make your readers want to know the main point of your paper, which you will state in the *thesis*. As you read works by professional historians, you may notice that the introduction to a journal article or book may be long, even several paragraphs, and the author's thesis may appear anywhere within it. Until you become skilled in writing about history, however, it is best to keep your introduction short and to state your thesis in the first paragraph.

The following is the first draft of the introductory paragraph for the paper on Harvey:

INEFFECTIVE

From ancient times, people have always been interested in the human body and how it works. Harvey was a seventeenth-century physician who performed many experiments and discovered the circulation of the blood.

This introduction begins with the ineffective opening sentence we looked at above. The "thesis statement" that follows isn't really a thesis at all; it is simply a statement of fact. (For more on writing an effective thesis, see 4c.) Moreover, there is no clear connection established between the ideas contained in the opening sentence and Harvey. From this first paragraph, a reader would have no idea what the paper was about, what its central point might be, or what to expect in the pages that follow.

In the final version of this introductory paragraph, the student uses the revised opening sentence and incorporates a more effective thesis, which is underlined here:

EFFECTIVE

For the scholars and physicians of seventeenth-century Europe, observations and experimentation began to replace authoritative texts as the most important source of information about human anatomy and physiology. This trend is clearly illustrated in the work of William Harvey, who designed controlled experiments to measure blood flow. However, <u>Harvey was not led to his revolutionary discovery of the circulation of the blood by experimentation alone, but was inspired by flashes of intuition and philosophical speculation.</u>

In this introductory paragraph, the connection between Harvey and the rise of observation and experiment in the seventeenth century is clear. Moreover, the thesis statement reflects the author's conclusions and anticipates the argument that will follow; we can expect that in the course of the paper, the author will support her argument by discussing Harvey's experimental method, his philosophical speculations, his moments of intuition, and the role all three played in his theories about circulation.

PLAN TO REWRITE YOUR OPENING PARAGRAPH. Because the opening paragraph plays such a crucial role in the overall effectiveness of your paper, you should always plan on revising it several times. In addition, when the paper is complete, it is important to check each section against the introduction. Does each paragraph provide evidence for your thesis? Is it clear to your reader how each point relates to the topic you have established in your introduction? Knowing that you will have to rewrite your introduction can be reassuring if you are having trouble beginning your paper. Write a rough, temporary opening paragraph, and return to it when you finish your first draft of the entire paper. The act of writing your draft will help you clarify your ideas, your topic, and your thesis.

4e-2. Writing clear and connected paragraphs

In your introduction, you present your subject and state your thesis. In the body of your paper, you provide an argument for your thesis based on evidence from the sources you have been reading and answer any objections that could be raised. You should think of each paragraph as a building block in your argument that presents *one* specific point. If the point of each paragraph is not clear, the reader will not be able to follow your reasoning and your paper will be weak and unconvincing. (For more on constructing an argument, see 4d.) The following advice will help you to write well-organized, cohesive, and persuasive paragraphs.

BEGIN EACH PARAGRAPH WITH A TOPIC SENTENCE. Each paragraph should have one driving idea which provides support for your paper's overall thesis. This idea or topic is usually asserted in the first sentence, or *topic sentence*. If you have made an outline, your topic sentences will be drawn from the list you made of the main points you wish to cover in your paper. (For advice on making an outline, see 5e.)

PROVIDE SUPPORT FOR THE PARAGRAPH'S MAIN POINT. The topic sentence should be followed by *evidence* from the text in the form of examples or statistics that supports the main point of the paragraph. Make sure that you do not wander off the point. If you include irrelevant information, you will lose momentum, and your readers will lose the thread of your argument. Instead, make sure you choose examples that provide clear and sufficient support for your main point. If you are using a direct quote as evidence, make sure you explain to the reader why you are including this quote by "framing" it in a way that shows how it supports your point. (For more information on how and when to quote, see Chapter 7).

MAKE CLEAR CONNECTIONS BETWEEN IDEAS. To be convincing, your evidence must be clear and well organized. Transitional words and phrases tell your readers how the individual statements in your paragraph are connected. To choose transitions that are appropriate, you will need to think about how your ideas are related to each other. Here are some transitional words or phrases that you might use to indicate particular kinds of relationships:

- **to compare:** *also, similarly, likewise*
- **to contrast:** *on the other hand, although, nevertheless, despite, on the contrary, still, yet, regardless, nonetheless, notwithstanding, whereas, however, in spite of*
- **to add or intensify:** *also, in addition, moreover, furthermore, too, besides, and*
- **to show sequence:** *first* (and any other numerical adjectives), *last, next, finally, subsequently, later, ultimately*
- **to indicate an example:** *for example, for instance, specifically*
- **to indicate cause-and-effect relationships:** *consequently, as a result, because, accordingly, thus, since, therefore, so*

WRITING PARAGRAPHS: AN EXAMPLE. Here is a paragraph from the first draft of a paper on Chinese relationships with foreigners during the Ming period:

INEFFECTIVE

The Chinese were willing to trade with barbarians. They distrusted foreigners. Jesuit missionaries were able to establish contacts in China. During the seventeenth century, they acquired the patronage of important officials. They were the emperor's advisers. Chinese women bound their feet, a practice that many Europeans disliked. Relations between China and Europe deteriorated in the eighteenth century. The Jesuits were willing to accommodate themselves to Chinese culture. Chinese culture was of great interest to the scholars of Enlightenment Europe. Matteo Ricci learned about Chinese culture and became fluent in Mandarin. He adopted the robes of a Chinese scholar. He thought that Christianity was compatible with Confucianism. The Jesuit missionaries had scientific knowledge. In the eighteenth century, the papacy forbade Chinese Christians to engage in any form of ancestor worship.

This paragraph is confusing. In the first place, it has no clear topic sentence; readers have to guess what the writer's main point is. This confusion is compounded by unclear connections between ideas; the paragraph lacks transitional words or phrases that alert readers to the connections that the writer sees between ideas or events. The paragraph is also poorly organized; the writer seems to move at random from topic to topic. Here is a revised version of the same paragraph:

EFFECTIVE

The Chinese of the Ming dynasty were deeply suspicious of foreigners; *nevertheless,* Jesuit missionaries were able to achieve positions of honor and trust in the imperial court, *ultimately* serving the emperor as scholars and advisers. At *first glance,* this phenomenon seems baffling; upon closer consideration, *however,* it becomes clear that the Jesuits' success was due to their willingness to accommodate themselves to Chinese culture. *For example,* one of the most successful of the early Jesuit missionaries, Matteo Ricci, steeped himself in Chinese culture *and* became fluent in Mandarin. To win the respect of the nobles, he *also* adopted the robes of a Chinese scholar. *Moreover,* he emphasized the similarities between Christianity and Chinese traditions. *Because* of their willingness to adapt to Chinese culture, Jesuit missionaries were accepted by the imperial court until the eighteenth century. Difficulties arose, *however,* when the papacy forbade Chinese Christians to engage in many traditional customs, including any form of ancestor worship. *As a result* of the church's increasing unwillingness to allow such practices, relations between China and Europe deteriorated.

This paragraph has been improved in several ways. First, a topic sentence, (which is underlined) has been added to the beginning. Readers no longer need to guess that this paragraph will address the apparent contrast between sixteenth-century Chinese suspicion of foreigners and the imperial court's acceptance of Jesuit missionaries.

Second, the author has clarified the connections between ideas by including transitional words and phrases. These transitions, (which are italicized) illustrate several different kinds of relationships, including contrast, cause and effect, sequence, and so on, and allow readers to follow the writer's argument.

Third, the paragraph has been reorganized so that the relationships between events are clearer. For example, the revised paragraph states explicitly that relations between China and European missionaries deteriorated in the eighteenth century because the church became less accommodating to Chinese customs, a relationship obscured in the original paragraph by poor organization.

Finally, the writer has removed references to foot binding and to interest in China during the Enlightenment. Both are interesting but irrelevant in a paragraph that deals with Chinese attitudes toward Europeans.

4e-3. Writing an effective conclusion

Your paper should not come to an abrupt halt, and yet you do not need to conclude by summarizing everything that you have said in the body of the text. Having read the entire paper, the reader will want to know "So what? Why is this important?" An effective conclusion answers these questions. Thus, it is usually best to end your paper with a paragraph that states the most important conclusions you have reached about your subject and the reasons you think those conclusions are significant.

NOTE: You should avoid introducing new ideas or information in the conclusion. If an idea or fact is important to your argument, you should introduce and discuss it earlier; if it is not, leave it out altogether.

The following is the first draft of the conclusion for the paper on Christian missionaries in China:

INEFFECTIVE

The Jesuit missionaries were sent to China in the Ming period. Some had good relationships with the emperor, but others didn't. Some learned Mandarin and dressed in court robes. The pope wouldn't let the Chinese worship their ancestors, but some Jesuits thought that Confucianism and Christianity were compatible. Another interesting aspect of Chinese culture at the time was the practice of footbinding.

This conclusion is ineffective for several reasons. First, there are no verbal clues to indicate that this is, in fact, the conclusion. In addition, it is too general and vague; which missionaries had good relationships with the emperor, and which didn't? Moreover, while it lists some of the key elements of the paper, it fails to indicate how these ideas are connected. Most important, perhaps, this conclusion does not suggest why the various ideas presented in the paper are important; it fails, in other words, to answer the questions "So what? Why is this important?" Finally, a new topic is introduced in the last sentence.

In the revised version of the conclusion, these problems have been addressed:

EFFECTIVE

Thus, it is clear that the success or failure of the Jesuits' missionary activity in China depended largely on the degree to which they were able to adapt to Chinese culture. The most successful missionaries learned Mandarin, adopted Chinese court dress, and looked for parallels between Christianity and the teachings of Confucius. It was only when the Church became more conservative — forbidding Chinese Christians, for example, to venerate their ancestors — that the Christian missionary effort in China began to fail. The experience of the Jesuit missionaries in China, then, provides an important clue about what determined the success or failure of missionary activity: Ultimately, cultural flexibility may have been a more effective religious ambassador than sophisticated theological arguments.

This conclusion has been improved in several ways. In the first place, it includes key transitional words (*thus,* *then*) that indicate that the writer is drawing conclusions. It reiterates the important elements of the paper's argument but leaves out information that is either very general ("the Jesuit missionaries were sent to China in the Ming period") or too vague ("some had good relationships with the emperor, but others didn't"). Moreover, unlike the earlier version, it is explicit about how the key topics in the paper — the flexibility of the Jesuit missionaries in adapting to Chinese culture, the parallels the missionaries drew between Christianity and Confucianism, and the institution of more conservative policies — are related. It does not add any new topics, however interesting those topics might be. And, most important, this version, unlike the first draft, clearly outlines the significance of the conclusions that the writer has reached: The Jesuit experience in China tells us something about the relationship between culture and religious belief.

4f. Revising your paper

One of the biggest mistakes that students make with any writing assignment is to leave themselves too little time to revise and edit their work. Although some students take a rather perverse pride in their ability to write a passable paper the night before it is due, the resulting work is never of the highest caliber and usually bears the hallmarks of careless writing: sloppy mistakes in reasoning, awkward constructions, poor word choice, lack of clear organization, and, of course, spelling and grammar mistakes. To write an effective history paper, you *must* allow yourself time to revise your paper.

When you revise, you need to read your paper critically, as if it were someone else's work. (For advice on critical reading, see 3a.) You should read for logic and clarity, making sure that your evidence is sufficient and that it supports your thesis. Be ruthless: Eliminate all extraneous material from the final draft of your paper, however interesting it may be. For instance, if you are writing about the role that Chinese laborers played in the westward expansion of the American railroads, do not spend three paragraphs discussing the construction of the steam locomotive. If your paper concerns the American government's treatment of Japanese citizens during World War II, do not digress into a discussion of naval tactics in the Pacific theater. You should also look for wordiness and awkward sentence structure, for repetition and cliché. (For advice on editing for word choice and grammar, see 4g). You must be willing to rearrange the order of material, do additional research to support weak points in your argument, and even change your entire thesis, if necessary. Obviously, you need to allow plenty of time for this part of the writing process, which may involve several drafts of the paper.

NOTE: As you revise, it is especially important to make sure that you have properly documented your work. All history papers, even a short essay, require that you cite and document the sources of your information. This is true even if your essay is an analysis of a single source; if you fail to cite your source or sources, you will be guilty of plagiarism. (See 6b for a discussion of when to cite sources. Models for how to document various kinds of historical sources can be found in 7d.)

4g. Considering word choice and grammar

When you revise your paper, you are considering the need for global changes: Does every part of the paper support the thesis, or is there extraneous material? Is the argument logical and cohesive, or does the paper need to be reorganized? Have I demonstrated my thesis, or does it need to be revised? etc. Once you have completed this process, you are ready for editing: the final stage of the writing process in which you focus on more limited issues like word choice and grammar.

It is essential that your writing follow the rules of formal English grammar. Historians are just as concerned as English professors with grammatical issues such as comma placement, subject-verb agreement, sentence fragments, misplaced modifiers, run-on sentences, and unclear antecedents. Grammar- and spell-check programs will help you avoid some mistakes, but they are no substitute for learning the rules. A spell checker, for example, will not pick up incorrectly used homophones (for example, *their, there,* and *they're*) or other words spelled correctly but used incorrectly. Always edit and proofread the final copy of your paper carefully; your instructor will not look kindly on a paper that is full of typographical, grammatical, and spelling errors.

It is beyond the scope of this manual to cover the basic rules of grammar. Any good style guide or writing manual will offer plenty of advice for writing clear grammatical sentences. (See Appendix A for a list of guides.) The following major points are useful to keep in mind when you write in history.

4g-1. Choosing appropriate language

While you must follow grammatical rules, you *do* have some flexibility when it comes to style, or the way in which you write (that is, simple or complex sentences; highly descriptive or stark; etc.). The way in which you express yourself and the words that you choose are a reflection of your own style. Nevertheless, there are some conventions governing word choice that historians follow that you will need to know in order to write effective history papers.

AVOID CONVERSATIONAL LANGUAGE, SLANG, AND JARGON. Because history papers are usually formal, you should use formal language rather than conversational language and slang. For example, although it is perfectly acceptable in conversational English to say that someone "was a major player" in an event, this expression is too informal for a history paper. In addition, slang often sounds anachronistic: Historians do not usually describe diplomats who fail to negotiate a treaty as having "struck out." Similarly, they describe ideas as archaic or outdated, not "so two minutes ago." Words with double meanings should be used only in their conventional sense; use *sweet* to refer to taste and *radical* to describe something extreme or on the political left. *Awesome* should generally be reserved for awe-inspiring things like Gothic cathedrals. You should also avoid jargon, or specialized language, which can often obscure your meaning.

Finally, contractions (for example, *wasn't* for "was not" or *won't* for "will not") are generally too informal for use in a history paper. Rather, you should use the expanded form.

NOTE: Computers have introduced many new words to the English language, but you should avoid misapplying them. For example, until the 1980s, people did not "access" documents or "download" information (and, if you are using books or journals, you are not "accessing" or "downloading" either – unless it is an online book or journal). Some other computer jargon to avoid includes the following:

- to interface (for "interact" or "discuss")
- to input (used as a verb, for "add or contribute information")
- databases (for "archives" or "document collections")
- to debug (for "to fix a problem")
- to process (for "to think about carefully" or "understand")

AVOID VALUE-LADEN WORDS. Historians, as noted earlier in this chapter (see 4b), attempt to understand the people of the past in their own contexts rather than judge them by the norms of the present. As a result, historians are especially careful to avoid not only anachronisms and generalizations but also value-laden language in their writing.

It is, of course, tempting to judge past events and people, particularly when they offend our own sense of values. For example, we might criticize the central figures of the American Revolution for their acceptance of slavery as an institution. Labeling these people as "racist" or "hypocritical" does not help us to understand, however, *what* they believed, *why* they believed it, or the social and cultural *context* in which they formed those beliefs. In this case, passing judgment on the people of the past does not help us to understand them or their society.

Other value-laden words that commonly find their way into history papers reflect the writer's sense that his or her own period, culture, and perceptions are superior to those of the past. Examples include: *backward, primitive, uncivilized,* and *superstitious.*

As you write about the past, then, it is important to consider the values that are implied in the words you use to describe your subject and to choose your words with care.

AVOID BIASED LANGUAGE. Always take care to avoid words that are gender-biased or that have negative connotations for particular racial, ethnic, or religious groups. You should never use expressions that are clearly derogatory. In addition, you should be aware that many words that were once acceptable are now deemed inappropriate. For example, the use of masculine words or pronouns to refer to both men and women, once a common practice, is now viewed as sexist by many. Use *humankind* or *people* rather than *mankind,* and do not use a masculine pronoun to refer to people of both genders.

In an attempt to avoid sexist language, students sometimes make a grammatical error instead. For example, in trying to eliminate the masculine pronoun *his* in the sentence "Each individual reader should form *his* own opinion," a student may write, "Each individual reader should form *their* own opinion." The problem with this new version is that the pronoun *their* is plural, while the antecedent, the word *reader,* is singular. The first version of the sentence is undesirable because it sounds sexist, and the second is unacceptable because it is ungrammatical. A grammatically correct revision is "Individual readers should form their own opinions." In this sentence, the antecedent (*readers*) and the pronoun (*their*) are both plural.

It is also important to realize that you cannot always rely on the books you are reading to alert you to biased language. The author of a fairly recent study of the origins of racism consistently refers to Asian people as "Orientals," a term that was not generally thought derogatory at the time of the book's publication. Since then, however, the word *Oriental* has come to be seen as having a Western bias and should therefore not be used. Another example is the term *Negro,* which once was a respectful term used to refer to people of African descent. Today, the preferred term is *black* or (for U.S. history) *African American.*

NOTE: You cannot correct the language of your sources. If you are quoting directly, you must use the exact wording of your source, including any racist or sexist language. If you are paraphrasing or summarizing a paragraph containing biased language, you might want to use unbiased language when it doesn't distort the sense of the source. Otherwise, put biased terms in quotation marks to indicate to your readers that the words are your source's and not yours.

MAKE YOUR LANGUAGE AS CLEAR AND SIMPLE AS POSSIBLE. In an effort to sound sophisticated, students sometimes use a thesaurus to find a more "impressive" word. The danger of this approach is that the new word might not mean what you intended. In general, you should use the simplest word that makes your meaning clear. Do not use a four-syllable word when a single syllable will do. Do not use five words (such as *due to the influence of*) where you can use one (*because*)

4g-2. Choosing the appropriate tense

The events that historians write about took place in the past; therefore, historians conventionally use the past tense. Students are sometimes tempted to use the historical present tense for dramatic effect, as in this example from a student paper:

INEFFECTIVE

The battle rages all around him, but the squire is brave and acquits himself well. He defends his lord fearlessly and kills two of the enemy. As the fighting ends, he kneels before his lord on the battlefield, the bodies of the dead and dying all around him. His lord draws his sword and taps it against the squire's shoulders. The squire has proven his worth, and this is his reward; he is now a knight.

This use of the present tense may be an effective device if you are writing fiction, but it is awkward in a history paper. First, readers might become confused about whether the events under discussion happened in the past or in the present, especially if the paper includes modern assessments of the issue. Second, use of the present makes it easy for the writer to fall prey to anachronism (see 4b). Perhaps more important, writing in the present sounds artificial; in normal conversation, we talk about events that happened in the past in the past tense. The same approach is also best for writing.

The present tense *is* used, however, when discussing the contents of documents, artifacts, or works of art because these still exist in the present. Note, for example, the appropriate use of past and present tenses in the following description:

EFFECTIVE

Columbus sailed across an "ocean sea" far greater than he initially imagined. The admiral's *Journal* tells us what Columbus thought he would find: a shorter expanse of water, peppered with hundreds of hospitable islands.

The events of the past are referred to in the past tense (*sailed, imagined, thought*), and the contents of the *Journal* are referred to in the present (*tells*).

The present tense is also used by historians when they are referring to the work of other scholars. Note, for example, this sentence from the annotated bibliography entry in Chapter 3: "Fletcher . . . argues that despite some productive interactions in the areas of trade and intellectual life, Christians and Muslims did not achieve any real measure of mutual understanding in the period under discussion."

4g-3. Using the passive voice sparingly

In general, historians prefer the use of active verbs, which express meanings more clearly and forcefully than verbs in the passive voice. In the *active voice,* the subject of the sentence is also the actor. These two examples illustrate the use of the active voice:

1. Duke William of Normandy conquered England in 1066.
2. By the seventh century, the Chinese had invented gunpowder, which they used to make fireworks.

In the *passive voice,* the subject of the sentence is not the actor but is acted on. The following sentences transform the previous examples into the passive voice:

1. England was conquered in 1066.
2. The process for making gunpowder was known in the seventh century.

Several difficulties arise when you use the passive voice. Persistent use of the passive voice can make writing sound dull and unnecessarily wordy. More important, however, the passive voice can obscure meaning and create unnecessary confusion. As you can see from the examples, readers cannot always tell who the actor is. We are not told who conquered England or who invented gunpowder. Use of the passive voice also allows writers to avoid the complexities of some historical issues. In the second example, moving from the passive to the active voice forces the writer to be more specific: The Chinese invented gunpowder, but they used it for making fireworks and not for firing weapons.

In addition, the use of the passive voice in expressions such as "it can be argued that" or "it has been argued that" is equivocal. The first expression suggests that the writer is unwilling to take responsibility for his or her arguments. If your evidence leads you to a certain conclusion, state it clearly. Using passive expressions like "it can be argued that" suggests that you are not really sure that your evidence is convincing. Similarly, the expression "it has been argued that" confuses readers: Who has made this argument? How many people and in what context? Readers must have this information to evaluate your argument. Moreover, use of this expression can result in plagiarism. If someone or several persons have argued a particular point, you should identify them in your text itself and in a citation.

This is not to say that you should never use the passive voice. Consider the following description of the Holocaust (verbs in the passive voice have been italicized):

> Hitler engaged in the systematic and ruthless murder of the Jewish people. In 1933, Jews *were forbidden* to hold public office; by 1935, they *were deprived* of citizenship. In all, over six million Jews *were killed* as part of Hitler's "final solution."

In this passage, the writer wants to draw the reader's attention to the recipients of the action — the six million Jews killed in the Holocaust. The persons acted on are more important than the actor. The passive voice, which focuses attention on the victims, is therefore appropriate.

The passive voice, then, can be effective, but it should be used only occasionally and for a specific reason.

4g-4. *Knowing when to use the pronouns* I, me, *and* you

Although you may occasionally see the pronouns *I, me,* and *you* in history books and journal articles, most professional historians use these pronouns sparingly, or not at all, and most instructors prefer students to avoid them whenever possible. However, a number of professors find their use not only acceptable but actually preferable to more labored constructions like "this evidence leads one to conclude that." Since the conventions governing the use of personal pronouns are in flux, it is best to consult your instructor about his or her preference. In any case, it is important to be consistent; if you use personal pronouns in the first paragraph ("My argument is based on the evidence of several primary sources"), don't switch to an impersonal construction in the second ("On the basis of the evidence, one might argue that . . .").

As noted at the beginning of this chapter, the conventions that historians follow in their writing are not a set of rules carved in stone, but historians read the work of their colleagues with certain expectations in mind. They assume that other historians will avoid anachronism and generalizations and respect the subjects of their writing. When they read a history paper, they look for a clearly articulated thesis and an argument in support of that thesis based on evidence. And, although they might not articulate these expectations, they follow conventions in their use of tense, voice, and word choice. Understanding and following these conventions will help you produce a paper that more closely conforms to the norms of the profession.

5
Writing a
Research Paper

A research paper, like a short essay, usually takes the form of an argument in support of a thesis based on evidence from sources. It is different from a short essay, however, in several ways. First, a research paper is more substantial, usually at least fifteen pages and often much longer. More important, a research paper requires that you go beyond the assigned readings for the course and engage in a significant amount of independent work. In order to write an effective research paper, you will need to formulate a research question; identify, locate, and gather sources that are pertinent to your topic; evaluate the credibility and usefulness of those sources and synthesize the information they contain; articulate a working thesis that asserts what you have concluded about the significance and meaning of the sources; develop an argument to support your thesis; and, finally, organize and present that argument in a systematic, clear, and appropriately documented fashion.

Your instructor might assign a specific research topic, or the choice might be left entirely up to you. Most often, you will be given some choice within a general area. The syllabus for a course with a research paper might, for example, include a statement like this in its list of course requirements:

> Research paper on any topic covered in the course, chosen in consultation with me. This paper should be 15–18 pages and is worth 40% of your final grade.

Students often find such assignments intimidating and may secretly yearn for an assigned subject; it often seems easier to write about a topic that holds no interest for you than to face the task of defining your own area of investigation. However, when you choose your own research topic, you are engaged in the practice of history at a much more sophisticated level. You are, in fact, doing the same work that a professional historian does: conducting research in order to answer the questions *you* have posed about a subject that *you* find compelling or problematic and then writing a paper that allows you to enter into a conversation with other scholars who are interested in similar questions and problems. The research paper, then, is both challenging and enormously exciting. It allows you, while still a student, to undertake original research and, perhaps, even discover something new. This, rather than its length, is what distinguishes the research project from other writing assignments.

Writing a research paper is an extremely complex activity; it does not proceed in a simple linear fashion, step-by-step. For the sake of clarity, this chapter divides the process of writing a research paper into the following stages: formulating the research question that you will answer in your paper; developing a research plan and a working thesis; conducting research; taking effective notes and writing an outline; and revising your paper. You should keep in mind, however, that real research involves a constant interaction of thinking, reading, and writing, and that the processes outlined in these sections will intersect and overlap.

5a. Formulating a research question

Deciding what topic to write about can seem overwhelming; out of an apparently infinite range of possibilities, how do you choose? The process is more manageable if you break it down into its component parts: choosing a broad subject that interests you, narrowing your focus to a topic that you will be able to write about in the time and space allotted, deciding what it is you want to know about the topic you have chosen to focus on, and, finally, formulating the research question that you want to answer in your paper.

5a-1. Choosing a subject

Since a research paper represents a significant investment of time and effort, you will produce your best work if you choose a topic that can sustain your interest over the course of an entire semester.

Start with the texts assigned for your class and find a general area that appeals to you. This might be a relatively wide-ranging subject, like "slavery and the Civil War." Obviously, this is much too broad to be the subject of your paper — you will not be able to write an effective essay on this subject within the length of a typical research paper — and you will ultimately need to narrow your focus to something much more specific. However, you will not know what problems, issues, and questions exist within the larger framework of the subject in which you are interested until you familiarize yourself with the research done by other scholars.

One way to begin to do this is to do some preliminary reading on the subject. You might start with a book assigned for your class. In addition, you might want to consult dictionaries, encyclopedias, and other general resources to get some background information about your subject. Such sources should never be primary sources of information for research papers at the college level, but reputable encyclopedias can provide useful background to get you started. (See Appendix B for a list of some reliable dictionaries, encyclopedias, and other resources in history.)

5a-2. Narrowing your subject to a workable topic

Narrowing a broad subject to a feasible topic for a research paper always begins with reading; however, simply reading everything you can find about "slavery and the Civil War" will *not* help you to narrow this subject to a suitable research topic. A history paper usually begins with a *question,* and you can begin to narrow your subject by rephrasing it as a series of questions. First, identify what it is that you want to know about "slavery and the Civil War." Are you interested in the role of abolitionists in the war? In the events and ideas that led up to the Emancipation Proclamation? In what slaves thought about the war? Then, having identified what it is that you hope to learn, you should be able to state your topic as a single question that you hope to answer as a result of your research, such as, What role did freed slaves play in Union regiments, and how were black soldiers treated by their white commanders? This research question should direct your reading.

As you read to find answers to the research question you have posed, you will gain a deeper knowledge of your topic — and more detailed and specific questions will arise. If you read actively in this way, constantly asking questions of the texts you are reading, you will discover which questions about your topic have been thoroughly discussed and which are less well studied. You will find the areas in which historians have reached consensus and questions that are still the subject of debate. Ultimately, you may even find an area where you feel you can say something both interesting and original — and thus enter into the scholarly debate yourself.

Finally, in developing your research question, you should determine what sources are available to you, either in your own college or university library, through interlibrary or consortium loans, or on the Internet. For example, you might decide that it would be interesting to examine the views of artisans during the French Revolution, but if you cannot obtain enough sources of information on this subject, this will not be a workable topic. Similarly, you should find out whether the sources for the topic in which you are interested are written in a language that you can read fluently. You might find that there are extensive collections of sources on artisans in revolutionary France — written in French. In this case, is your command of the language sufficient for the research you hope to pursue?

5b. Developing a research plan

The previous section has hinted at the effort you will need to put into gathering, reading, and evaluating texts as you move from selecting a subject to narrowing your subject to a workable topic and developing a research question. Obviously, a research paper is a serious scholarly endeavor; it cannot be done effectively at the last minute. Sometimes, your professor might break the research process into phases for you. You might be asked to produce a written topic proposal, an annotated bibliography, an outline, and a rough draft of your paper as separate graded assignments. In this case, much of the time-management difficulties involved in the production of a research paper will have been done for you. More often, you will need to develop a research plan for yourself.

In planning your research strategy, you should consider what information you will need at each stage of the process, what sources you will need to consult in order to acquire that information, where you can find those sources, and how much time you will need to allow for research. Your research plan should reflect the subject you have chosen. For example, if the subject on which you are writing is obscure, locating sources may take significantly more time than if you are writing about a relatively well-known subject. In the first case, you would probably need to allocate more time to evaluating primary sources that have not been well studied, while in the second instance, you would need more time to read and evaluate what other scholars have said. In either case, you would need to allow enough time to find and gather the materials needed; develop a working bibliography; read, evaluate, and take notes on your sources; and formulate a working thesis.

Start your research early. The day you receive the assignment is not too soon to begin. The importance of starting early becomes obvious once you realize that Internet sources, while often very useful and readily available, are *not* sufficient for a research paper. You will also need to consult books, journal articles, and other print materials. Therefore, it is always safest to anticipate problems in gathering your sources: Other people may have borrowed the books you want, or you may have to travel to other libraries or archives to use their collections. If you are interested in a topic for which your own library has only limited sources, you might be able to borrow books from other colleges and universities on interlibrary loan. But to ensure that you get your books in time, you will need to make your request early.

5b-1. Gathering and managing sources

Once you have decided on a topic, begin to gather sources for your paper. Students often make the mistake of photocopying every article and ordering every book they can find on their subject. Merely collecting stacks of photocopies and piles of books will not move you forward in the process of writing a research paper. Instead, you will need to develop a strategy for finding *useful* sources and managing your organization and synthesis of the material they contain. The following advice will help you gather and work with your sources in an efficient and intelligent manner.

IDENTIFY BOTH PRIMARY AND SECONDARY SOURCES. A good research paper contains references to a variety of sources. Sometimes, your professor might specify the number and kind of sources he or she expects you to use. Usually, you will need to consult primary sources (letters, diaries, original documents, and so on) from the period you are studying. You will also need to consult secondary sources to become familiar with the ways in which other historians have interpreted this material. Your secondary sources should reflect a balance of materials. While books are valuable sources, you should not confine your research to books; important recent research is often found in articles in scholarly journals. You will probably find both primary and secondary sources on the Internet; however, you should note that *Internet sources alone are not sufficient for a research paper*. In any case, you should evaluate the usefulness and reliability of your sources as you read, using the criteria set out in Chapter 2. Finally, as you begin to gather sources, always keep your research question in mind. If you allow yourself to be sidetracked by fascinating material that is not related to your research question, you will not be able to finish your paper on time.

USE NONWRITTEN MATERIALS WHERE APPROPRIATE. Although much of the work you do in an undergraduate history course will depend on the reading and interpretation of written sources, historians also use a wide variety of nonwritten sources in their work. The following types of nonwritten materials may be useful to you in researching and writing your paper:

- *Maps* are especially useful when you are trying to explain geographical relationships, such as the movements of troops during a battle or the changes in the national boundaries of a particular area over time.

- *Graphs and charts* are useful for illustrating statistical information, such as rates of marriages, births, or deaths and changes in per capita income over a particular period of time.
- *Photographs, cartoons, and other illustrations* may provide evidence that supports or contradicts the written sources, or may provide a unique perspective on events.
- *Diagrams,* such as a sketch of the west portal of Chartres cathedral or architectural plans illustrating the floor plan and elevation of the Empire State Building, can help the reader understand how parts are related to a larger whole.

KEEP A WORKING BIBLIOGRAPHY. As you gather sources for your research, you should keep a working bibliography in which you record complete bibliographic information for every item you have examined. (See 7d for a description of the elements that constitute complete bibliographic information.) Nothing is more frustrating than to return all your books to the library only to discover that you are missing authors' names, dates of publication, or other information you will need for your bibliography. You should also record complete bibliographical information for any nonwritten sources you examine or cite. If you have not written many academic papers, you may find it difficult to remember all of the elements that should be included in a bibliographic entry; therefore, while doing your research, you may want to keep this guide handy. Or you may find it useful to list the information you need to record on an index card that you can carry with you.

NOTE: Do not make generating a bibliography an end in itself. You still need to read the books and articles you have found! Your final bibliography should include only the materials you have read and found useful in writing your paper.

5b-2. Developing a working thesis

The role the thesis plays in a history paper has already been discussed in some detail in Chapter 4. In a research paper, where the writer has to pose his or her own research question and conduct significant independent

work, the role of the thesis is particularly crucial. All of
the preliminary reading that you do for your research
paper and the writing that attends that reading (listing
questions, taking notes, jotting down ideas, etc.) is intended to stimulate and clarify your thinking. The result
of all of this thinking and reading and writing is the gen-
eration of a working thesis: a single sentence in which
you suggest a tentative answer to your research question.
From this point on, your research process should center
on this working thesis. All of the sources you plan to include in your paper should provide evidence to support it
or help you respond to arguments that might be raised
against it.

Keep in mind, however, that the thesis at this stage in
the production of a research paper is only a *working* thesis. As you gather, read, and evaluate texts, organize your
notes, develop ideas about your topic, and begin to write
the paper itself, it is important to remain flexible. Your
working thesis should lead to additional reading, and the
evidence you uncover in the course of that reading must
always lead you to test your thesis – does it still hold up
as you find out new information or encounter new interpretations? Willingness to modify your thesis in response
to your research is the hallmark of a good historian.

5c. Conducting research

In order to articulate a research question, you will need
to identify and evaluate a substantial number of primary
and secondary sources of various types. Moreover, once
you have developed a working thesis, you will need to
conduct even more research to refine and test it. But how
do you go about finding the sources you will need to
write an effective research paper? This section provides
some suggestions for how to use print and electronic research tools to locate reliable sources from among the
wealth of materials available to you.

5c-1. Consulting human resources

Technology has become such a part of most students'
lives that they may instinctively begin a research project
by going online. However, you will save a great deal of
time and effort if you begin by consulting two very important human resources.

BEGIN BY CONSULTING YOUR PROFESSOR. Although a research paper may seem daunting to you, you should remember that your professor has had a great deal of experience in conducting research and writing papers and is intimately familiar with the research produced by other historians. Take advantage of this expertise by utilizing office hours, chat rooms, websites, and other forums for consulting your professor. He or she will be delighted by your interest and will be happy to point you in a number of potentially fruitful directions. Ask your professor to recommend books and articles on your topic, and make sure you consult these at the outset of your research. Your professor can also direct you to the most important scholarly journals in the field you are researching.

CONSULT A REFERENCE LIBRARIAN. Reference librarians are invaluable resources that are too often overlooked. They are extremely helpful in tracking down important print and electronic journals, bibliographies, book reviews, and other research tools. Reference librarians can also teach you how to search your university's online catalog and how to use the databases to which your university subscribes.

5c-2. Using the library's online catalog

Having consulted your professor and a research librarian, you should start your own search for sources in your university's library. Begin by acquainting yourself with the library itself. Locate the stacks and reference room; find out if your library has microfilm or microfiche materials; determine if there is a rare book room. Many universities also have archives that you might want to access for special projects. Then, familiarize yourself with your library's online catalog.

Each library's homepage is unique; however, typically it provides information that will enable you to find the print resources that are available in your own library as well as links to a variety of electronic sources, including databases, reference sources, journals, subscription-only services, and e-texts. Most homepages also provide access to the Internet and links to other college and university libraries. The library homepage of my own university, Trinity (Washington) University, shows the kinds of information you could expect to find (see Figure 5.1).

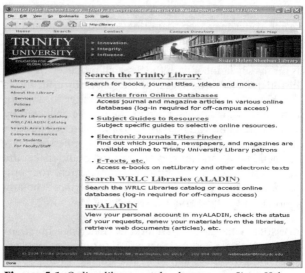

Figure 5.1 Online library catalog homepage, Sister Helen Sheehan Library, Trinity (Washington) University

At the beginning of a research project, you should search your library's online catalog to find out what sources are available in your own library. These usually include books, scholarly journals, audio and/or video recordings, CD-ROMs, and microform/microfilm materials (such as back issues of newspapers). If your library has a card catalog, be sure to check it as well; some college libraries are still in the process of computerizing their holdings, and you may overlook important sources if you rely solely on the online catalog.

Typically, you can search an online catalog by author, title, subject, or keyword. If your professor has recommended a specific book, searching by title or author is simple and efficient. You can then find other books of interest by browsing the shelves in the area where your book is housed because books on the same topic are grouped together. Also consult the bibliographies and notes of any useful books you find; these will lead you to other primary and secondary sources of interest.

If you don't have a particular book in mind, you can conduct a "subject" or "keyword" search. Keep in mind, however, that a subject search reflects the formal Library of Congress subject listings, which may not always be obvious. It is usually best to try a keyword search, using as many keywords as you can think of that might lead you to materials on your topic. For example, you might look for materials on the medieval plague by entering "bubonic plague," "Black Death," and "Black Plague," each of which would yield slightly different results. You can search the online catalog most effectively by conducting an advanced or guided keyword search which allows you to include or exclude specific terms in your search parameters. For example, if you wanted to examine the plague in continental Europe in the fourteenth century, you could limit your search to "Black Death" AND "14th century" but NOT "England." Your online catalog will provide instructions for conducting a guided keyword search, and the time you invest in learning how to do this will make your search much more efficient.

Unless you attend a major research university, you might want to expand your search to other institutions' holdings. Often, your library's homepage will include links to local colleges and universities whose catalogs you can also search online. For example, Trinity's library homepage includes links to the Washington Research Library Consortium (WRLC) and to other area libraries, which allow students to search the catalogs of universities in the greater Washington metropolitan area. If you find materials of interest, you can usually order them through interlibrary loan; increasingly, articles can be sent by electronic file to your library or even directly to your own e-mail address. Finally, your library's homepage may include a link to e-texts, books available online. Clearly, then, you can use the online catalog of your university's library to open up a much broader research base.

5c-3. Using print and electronic reference sources

As noted in section 5a, you may want to consult a variety of print and electronic reference sources at the beginning of your research process. Useful sources include encyclopedias (both general, such as the *Encyclopaedia Britannica*, and specialized, such as *The Encyclopedia of the Vietnam War*); topical and biographical dictionaries (such as *The Historical Dictionary of the Elizabethan World* or *The New Dictionary of National Biography*); chronologies; and atlases. Keep in mind that you should look for both print and electronic sources. You will find print sources in your library's reference room. The library's homepage will typically provide links to reliable online reference sources as well, some of which are available only by subscription and must therefore be accessed at the library rather than through your own computer. Sometimes, these sources may be organized for you by subject. For example, your library may provide a research guide for history that lists links to electronic resources of interest to historians. Several important print and online reference works are listed in Appendix B.

NOTE: Some encyclopedias are available online, but they are not all equally reliable. One popular online encyclopedia, *Wikipedia,* allows any reader to add or edit entries. Consequently, the entries cannot be assumed to be accurate. Before you use an Internet reference source, make sure you know who has written the entries and what organization sponsors the website. Better still, use the links on your library's homepage to guide you to appropriate online reference sources.

5c-4. Using print and electronic periodical databases

Articles in scholarly journals are extremely important sources for students embarking on a research project. Recently published articles not only represent the most up-to-date work on the topic in which you are interested, but they frequently contain an overview of the academic work on the subject and provide references to other important books and articles. Nevertheless, while students usually have no trouble finding books, locating relevant journal articles can be a bit more difficult. Typically, the online catalog will list the journals (both print and electronic) to which your library subscribes — but how do you find the articles that are of interest to you? You can, of course, use the bibliographies in the books you have found to identify appropriate journal articles. If you want to conduct a thorough search, though, you will need to use print and electronic bibliographies, indexes, and periodical databases to help you locate useful articles. Several of these are listed in Appendix B.

Most scholarly journals provide annual print or electronic indexes, organized by author, title, and subject, which you will find in your library's reference room. An increasing number of scholarly journals bypass print entirely and are published online; several of these journals of special interest to historians are listed in Appendix B. In addition, your library's homepage will direct you to databases such as *LexisNexis Academic, JSTOR, Project Muse,* and *Pro-Quest,* that can help you locate journal articles. Sometimes, these databases will contain abstracts of articles, giving you some idea about the content; if an article looks promising, you can request a copy through interlibrary loan or as an electronic file delivered by e-mail. Other databases provide access to full-text articles.

While electronic databases have greatly expanded the ability of students to find and access scholarly work, it is important to be aware of their limitations. For example, Project Muse (http://muse.jhu.edu/) provides online access to over 300 journals in the humanities, arts, and social sciences. It keeps an archive of its journals once they go online but does not have issues that predate online posting. In many cases, older articles are still useful, and students will need to find them by using print indexes. In contrast, *JSTOR: The Scholarly Journal Archive* (http://www .jstor.org), attempts to make available a complete back run of all of its 600+ participating journals. It does not, however, provide access to current issues. (Typically, its archive is between one to five years behind the current publication date.) It is important, then, to know the date range of the database you are using. Finally, note that many of these excellent research tools are only available by subscription. *You will not be able to access many of these databases from your own computer,* and if your university has not purchased a license, you will not be able to access them at your library either.

5c-5. Locating primary sources

Primary sources are the essential materials with which historians work, and you will find primary sources in print and electronic formats. Book-length sources, like novels, chronicles, and memoirs, are available in print, either in their original form or in editions and translations (see Chapter 2 for advice on how to evaluate translations and editions of primary sources). Many are also available online as e-texts. You may be able to examine original primary sources like letters, diaries, wills, or photographs directly at an archive; more commonly, you will be using document collections that have been organized for you by an editor. Such collections are also available online. In addition, you can find government documents and newspapers, both current and archived, from around the world on the Internet. Specialized primary source collections for virtually every historical period worldwide can also be found on the Internet. In order to locate these collections, you may want to begin with a general history internet site, like *Academic Info History Gateway* (http://www.academicinfo.com/hist.html), or refer to a reference book like Dennis Trinkle and Scott Merriman's *The History Highway 3.0: A Guide to Internet Resources*. Several other valuable collections of primary sources on the Web are included in Appendix B and in the appendices of the Internet guides listed in Appendix A.

NOTE: As you look for primary sources on the Internet, keep in mind that to abide by copyright laws, some websites, particularly those dealing with older materials, may post editions or translations of sources that are in the public domain. (A reputable website will inform you if this is the case.) Editions that are in the public domain were made so long ago that they are no longer covered by copyright restrictions. In such cases, the Internet is still an extremely useful tool for making you aware of the wide variety of sources that are available, but once you find a source you intend to use, you will probably want to look elsewhere for the most recent printed edition or translation. Moreover, many primary and secondary sources are not yet available on the Internet. Students who rely solely on electronic media will miss many fundamental and indispensable sources. It is vital, therefore, that you consult both electronic and print sources in your research.

5c-6. Using Internet search tools

As a result of the rapid expansion of the Internet, the amount of research material available to any individual student has multiplied exponentially. As you move outside your library's electronic environment onto the Internet, make sure you use caution. Virtually anyone with a computer, a modem, and the right software can create a website. As a result, many websites are useless for serious research; it is essential, therefore, that you carefully evaluate the websites that you access. Nonetheless, the Internet is a worthwhile tool for research. This section will introduce you to a few online research techniques that can make your Internet searches more effective.

When you look for information on the Internet, you will usually use a search engine like *Google* or *Yahoo!* A number of search engines are listed in Appendix B. Whichever search engine you choose, spend some time determining what choices are available for conducting a search. For example, in most instances, you will be able to choose either to conduct a keyword search or to search a directory that offers a list of categories with increasingly specialized subcategories. In addition, most search engines provide the option of specialized searches, such as searching for images or searching within a particular topic. *Google "Scholar,"* one specialized option of *Google*, allows you to look only for scholarly materials such as peer-reviewed articles from academic publishers.

An Internet search using a search engine will be most fruitful if you keep the following advice in mind:

Tips for Writers

Conducting an Internet Search

- If you do a keyword search, use the same techniques that you apply to a keyword search of your university's online catalogue, trying as many keywords as you can think of that will yield information on your topic.

- Learn how to conduct an advanced search in order to limit the number of results; a search that yields a million hits will not be terribly useful.

- Keep in mind that although many search engines try to sort their results by relevance, the search engine is not always perfect. The first few hits may be useless, while the seventeenth is just what you need.

- When you search using a directory, you should think creatively about the categories with which your topic might be associated. In *Yahoo!*, for example, "History" is a subcategory of "Humanities," which itself is a subcategory of "Arts," the "*Yahoo!* Web Directory" category that appears on the *Yahoo!* homepage. If you don't find your topic on the first try, go back and try a different category until you find what you are looking for.

- It is commonly assumed that search engines search the Internet: They *do not*. Rather, they search a *database*. Since each search engine uses a different database, it is essential to use several search engines for the best possible results. In addition, you might use a metasearch engine such as *MetaCrawler*, which will run your search terms through several search engines at once.

Conducting an Internet Search, continued

- Always evaluate the reliability of any website you find using the criteria outlined in section 2b-3. When you find a useful and reliable website, use the links provided to find additional materials.

- Always bookmark useful sites so that you can return to them for more careful study at a later date. Your bibliography must include complete bibliographical information about any websites you use.

The Internet can be a double-edged sword. On the one hand, students should be aware that Internet sources are not sufficient for historical research; they will always need to consult books and scholarly articles. Moreover, the Internet is fraught with misinformation in the form of unreliable websites. On the other hand, used with care and with a critical eye, the Internet can be an invaluable supplement to the student-researcher, providing access to a wide variety of sources that would otherwise be unavailable. If you begin with your university's library and its online catalog and move onto the Internet from there, you will be able to make the most of this invaluable tool in your own research.

5d. Taking effective research notes

Your final paper will only be as good as the notes you take. There is no right or wrong way to take notes for a research paper. Many people favor index cards that can be arranged and rearranged easily. Others prefer to use notebooks or legal pads. If you have a laptop computer, you may wish to type your notes directly into an electronic file. This can be especially useful if you use a word processing program with a global search function so that you can use the search command to find keywords quickly wherever they appear in your notes. But whatever method you use, there are several things you can do to make your note taking more effective.

WRITE AS YOU READ. Most scholars would agree that reading and writing are interactive processes. The writing you do while reading can take many different forms. If you own some of the books you are using for your paper, or if you have made photocopies of some of the important materials you will be using, you might want to write directly on the text, underlining important points and writing comments in the margins. Develop your own code for marginal notation so that you will be able to identify arguments that you find questionable, insights that you find important, or words that you need to define. (For further suggestions on writing as you read, see Chapter 3). You should also write notes to yourself about any ideas, insights, or questions that occur to you as you read. This writing will help you clarify your thoughts about what you are reading and provide direction for your research.

ALWAYS RECORD COMPLETE BIBLIOGRAPHIC INFORMATION FOR YOUR SOURCES. It is absolutely essential that you be able to identify the source of any facts, ideas, maps, graphs, or quotations that you derive from your research, and that you clearly differentiate the ideas of others from your own. Careful note taking will save you lots of time tracking down quotations and will ensure that you do not plagiarize inadvertently.

TAKE MOST OF YOUR NOTES IN THE FORM OF SUMMARIES. If you take notes word for word from your source, you are simply acting as a human photocopier. Your goal should be to digest the information presented in your sources and make it your own. It is much more useful to read carefully and thoughtfully, close the book, and summarize in your own words the section you have read. Then compare your summary with the original, noting any important points that you missed or anything that you misunderstood. At this point, you should also check carefully to make sure that you have not inadvertently taken any words or phrases directly from the original text. This type of note taking not only will ensure that you really understand the material but also will help you avoid plagiarism.

COPY QUOTATIONS ACCURATELY. If you do decide to quote directly from a source, make sure you copy the words and punctuation exactly, and always use quotation marks so that you will know it is a direct quote when you return to your notes. Do not try to improve the wording of the original or correct the spelling or grammar. You may, however, alert your readers to an error in spelling or grammar by recording the error as it appears in the source and then noting the mistake by adding the Latin word *sic* in brackets: "Do not correct mispelled [sic] words."

AVOID THE MISCONCEPTION THAT "TO PHOTOCOPY IS TO KNOW." Photocopying material on your topic is no substitute for reading and understanding it. Photocopying doesn't save time; in fact, unless you are photocopying important sources so that you can annotate them, it is often a waste of time. Eventually, you will have to read and interpret the photocopied material, and when you do, you may notice that you have copied irrelevant material and missed important information.

5e. Making an outline

Note taking, however precise and clear, is not an end in itself. The notes you take should be directed toward providing the information that will allow you to refine and support your working thesis as you attempt to answer your research question. If you have taken careful notes while conducting research, you will be able to organize them into an outline in which you sketch out the body of your paper.

The most important function of an outline is to provide a guide that identifies the points you wish to cover and the order in which you plan to cover them. A good outline will help you present the evidence that supports your thesis as a convincing argument. Some students have been trained to write formal outlines with roman numerals and various subheadings. If this method works for you, by all means use it. Many students find formal outlines too constraining and prefer instead to write a less formal outline. You might begin an informal outline by writing down the main points you want to discuss. These will form the topic sentences of paragraphs. Underneath each main point, list the evidence that supports it. Outlining your paper in this way will reveal any points that require additional evidence. It will also help ensure that your evidence is organized in a logical and orderly manner and that each idea is connected to those that precede and follow it.

Finally, remember that an outline is a *tool*. As you continue to think and write about your subject, you may discover new material or change your mind about the significance of the material you have examined. You may even change your thesis (which is why your thesis at this stage is still a *working* thesis rather than a *final* one). When this happens, you must be willing to revise your outline too.

If you have taken careful and thorough notes and organized them effectively in an outline, what originally seemed to be a daunting task will become much more manageable. The advice in Chapter 4 on following the conventions of writing history papers will provide guidance as you draft your research paper.

5f. Revising and editing your paper

The word *revise* comes from the Latin *revisere,* which means "to look at again." When you revise a paper, you are, quite literally, looking at the paper again with critical eyes. As you revise, think about whether you have organized your argument in the most effective manner. You should also determine whether you have presented enough evidence to support your thesis. You may even decide at this stage that you need to conduct additional research; this is one way in which revising a research paper differs from revising a short essay. Most importantly, you should reexamine your thesis in light of the evidence you have provided, evaluate the validity of that thesis, and modify or change it completely if necessary. (For more advice on revising your paper, see 4f.) Finally, once your revision is complete, you will need to edit your paper to correct grammatical and typographical errors. (Additional advice on word choice and grammar can be found in 4g.)

A research paper is a complex project. It is unrealistic to expect that one or two drafts will be sufficient to do justice to it. As you plan your research, make sure you leave yourself sufficient time to revise and edit thoroughly. Obviously, a research paper represents a significant commitment of time, effort, and intellect. Nonetheless, the rewards are equally great, for it is in the research paper that students can experience the pleasures of truly original interpretation and discovery.

6
Plagiarism: What It Is and How to Avoid It

Plagiarism is the act of taking the words, ideas, or research of another person and putting them forward without citation as if they were your own. It is intellectual theft and a clear violation of the code of ethics and behavior that most academic institutions have established to regulate the scholastic conduct of their members. Most colleges and universities have their own policies that define plagiarism and establish guidelines for dealing with plagiarism cases and punishing offenders, but the penalties for plagiarism are usually severe, ranging from an automatic F in the course to temporary suspension or even permanent expulsion from the school. Plagiarism, in short, is considered a very serious academic offense.

If we look simply at the dictionary definition, it would seem that acts of plagiarism are readily identifiable. And, indeed, some instances of plagiarism are obvious; deliberately copying lengthy passages from a book or journal article, submitting an essay written by a classmate as your own, or purchasing or downloading whole papers and submitting them as your own work, are clear-cut examples of plagiarism. However, although some students unfortunately make a conscious decision to plagiarize, many more do so inadvertently. This is because, unlike the instances cited above, some situations in which you might use the words or ideas of another may seem murkier. Because of its seriousness, it is essential that you know exactly what kinds of acts constitute plagiarism.

This chapter will clarify the concept and give you some advice on how to avoid unintentional plagiarism.

6a. What is plagiarism?

Read the following scenarios. Which of these would be considered plagiarism?

- A student borrows a friend's essay to get some ideas for his own paper. With his friend's permission, he copies portions of it, taking care, however, to cite all the sources his friend included in the original.
- A student finds useful information on a website that is not under copyright. She downloads and incorporates sections of this website into her paper, but does not cite it since it is in the public domain.
- A student derives some key ideas for his paper from a book. Since he doesn't quote anything directly from this book, he doesn't provide any footnotes. He does, however, include the book in his bibliography.
- A student modifies the original text by changing some words, leaving out an example, and rearranging the order of the material. Since she is not using the exact words of the original, she does not include a footnote.

The answer is that *all four* of these scenarios illustrate examples of plagiarism.

In the first instance, the issue is not whether the student has permission from his friend to use his or her work. As long as the student is submitting work done by another as his own, it is plagiarism. Citing the sources that his friend has used does not mitigate the charge of plagiarism. In the second example, the fact that the student has used material that is not protected by copyright is irrelevant. She is guilty of plagiarism because she has submitted the words of another as her own. The third instance illustrates that the definition of plagiarism encompasses not only the use of someone else's words, but also of their ideas; you must *always* acknowledge the source of your ideas in a footnote or endnote, even if you specifically include the text in your bibliography. Finally, in the fourth example, changing some of the words, reorganizing the material, or leaving out some phrases does not constitute a genuine paraphrase; moreover, even an effective paraphrase requires a footnote.

As a history student you are part of a community of scholars; when you write history papers, you become part of the intellectual conversation of that community. The published words and ideas of other historians are there to be used — but as a matter of intellectual honesty, you are bound to acknowledge their contributions to your own thought.

6b. Avoiding plagiarism

Most unintentional plagiarism can be traced to three sources: confusion about when and how to cite sources, uncertainty about how to paraphrase, and carelessness in taking notes and downloading Internet materials.

6b-1. Citing sources to avoid plagiarism

When you derive facts and ideas from other writers' work, you must cite the sources of your information. Most writers are aware that they must cite the sources of direct quotations. However, students sometimes assume, erroneously, that direct quotations are the *only* things they need to cite. In fact, "borrowing" ideas from other writers without documenting them is a form of plagiarism every bit as serious as taking their words. Therefore, you must provide citations for *all* information derived from another source, even if you have summarized or paraphrased the information. Furthermore, you must also cite your sources when you use other writers' interpretations of a historical event or text. In short, you should remember that any time that you use information derived from another person's work, adopt someone else's interpretation, or build on another writer's ideas, you must acknowledge your source. This enables your readers to distinguish between your ideas and those of others.

The only exception is that you do not need to provide citations for information that is common knowledge. For example, you might have learned from a particular book that the Civil War spanned the years 1861 to 1865, but you do not have to cite the book when you include this fact in your paper. You could have obtained the time span of the Civil War from any number of sources because it is common knowledge. The more you read about your subject, the easier it will be for you to distinguish common knowledge from information that needs a citation. When in doubt, however, it is better to be safe and cite the source. (For additional information on quoting and citing sources, including documentation models, see Chapter 7.)

NOTE: One practice that will help you to avoid plagiarism is to keep all of your research notes and rough drafts in separate files. Then, as you prepare your final draft, you will be able to check your notes if you are uncertain about whether a particular phrase is a direct quote or a paraphrase, or where an idea or quotation came from. (See 5d for more on careful note taking.)

6b-2. Paraphrasing to avoid plagiarism

Most students know that copying a passage word for word from a source is plagiarism. However, many are unsure about how to paraphrase. Consider, for example, this passage from a textbook and the student "paraphrase" that follows:

ORIGINAL PASSAGE

In the early twentieth century, most Latin American nations were characterized by two classes separated by a great gulf. At the top were a small group of European-descended white people, the *patrones* (landlords or patrons), who, along with foreign investors, owned the ranches, mines and plantations of each nation. Like the established families of most societies elsewhere in the world, the *patrones* monopolized the wealth, social prestige, education, and cultural attainments of their nations. Many of them aspired to the ideal of nobility, with high standards of personal morality and a parental concern for those who worked for them. Some *patrones* lived up to these ideals, but most, consciously or unconsciously, exploited their workers.[1]

UNACCEPTABLE PARAPHRASE

In the early part of this century most Latin American countries were typified by two classes separated by a large chasm. At the top were a small group of white people, de-

---

1. Richard Goff, Walter Moss, Janice Terry, and Jiu-Hwa Upshur, *The Twentieth Century: A Brief Global History,* 4th ed. (New York: McGraw-Hill, 1994), 62.

scended from Europeans, called *patrones.* Along with foreign investors, the *patrones* owned the plantations,
ranches, and mines of their countries. Like aristocrats all
over the world, the *patrones* controlled the wealth, social
status, education, and cultural achievements of their
countries. Many of them had high standards of morality
and were concerned for their workers, but most, consciously or unconsciously, abused their workers.

In this example, the writer's attempt at paraphrase results
in plagiarism, *despite the fact* that the second text is not an
exact copy of the original. The writer has used a thesaurus
to find synonyms for several words — *characterized* has become *typified, gulf* has been replaced by *chasm,* and
achievements has been substituted for *attainments.* In addition, several words or phrases in the original have been left
out in the second version, and the word order has occasionally been rearranged. Nevertheless, these changes are
merely editorial; the new paragraph is not significantly different from the original in either form or substance.

NOTE: This paragraph would be considered plagiarism
even if the writer acknowledged the source of the material;
it is simply too close to the original to be considered the
work of the student.

In a genuine paraphrase, the writer has thought about
what the source says and absorbed it. Once the writer un-
derstands the content of the source, he or she can restate
it in an entirely original way that reflects his or her own
wording and style. Consider, for example, this paraphrase:

ACCEPTABLE PARAPHRASE

The society of Latin America at the beginning of this century was sharply divided into two groups: the vast majority of the population, made up of the workers, and a
wealthy minority, the *patrones,* who were descended from
white Europeans. Although the *patrones* represented a very
small segment of the population, they controlled the
lion's share of their countries' wealth and enjoyed most of
the social and educational advantages. Like their counterparts in Europe, many *patrones* adopted an attitude of pa-
ternalistic benevolence toward those who worked for
them. Even if their concern was genuine, however, the *patrones* clearly reaped the rewards of their workers' labor.[2]

2. Goff, et al., 62.

This paraphrase is more successful; the writer has assimilated the content of the source and expressed it in his own words.

NOTE: Even though this is an acceptable paraphrase of the original, and although there are no direct quotations used, the author would still need to provide a citation, like the footnote in this example, indicating the source of this information.

You will save time if you paraphrase as you take notes. However, if you attempt to paraphrase with the original source open in front of you, you are courting disaster. To write a genuine paraphrase, you should close the book and rewrite in your own words what you have read. (For advice on taking notes in the form of summaries, see p. 85. A shorter example of paraphrasing can be found on p. 97.)

Tips for Writers

Rules for Avoiding Plagiarism

If . . .	Then . . .
The information is common knowledge	You do not need a citation.
The *words* are your own AND the *idea* is your own	You do not need a citation.
The *words* are someone else's	Place them in quotation marks AND include a citation.
The *words* are your own BUT the *idea* is someone else's	Acknowledge the author of the idea by referring to him or her in the text AND include a citation.

NOTE This chart also appears in "Academic Honesty, Plagiarism, and the Honor System: A Handbook for Students," (Trinity [Washington] University, 2005), 2, and is reprinted by permission.

6b-3. Downloading Internet sources carefully to avoid plagiarism

As with any other source, information derived from the Internet must be properly paraphrased and cited. A particular danger arises, however, from the ease with which Internet material can be downloaded into your working text. Whenever you download material from the Internet, be sure to create a *separate* document file for that material. Otherwise, Internet material may inadvertently become mixed up with your own writing. Moreover, you should keep in mind that Internet sites are more volatile than print sources. Material on many Internet sites is updated on a daily basis, and a site that you find early in your research may be gone by the time you write your final draft. Therefore, you should always record *complete* bibliographic information for each Internet source *as you use it.*

6c. Plagiarism and the Internet

While plagiarism is not a new problem, the opportunities for plagiarism have increased exponentially with the growing popularity of and dependence on the Internet. Careless "cut and paste" note taking poses a real hazard to unwary Internet users. A more distressing and significant problem, however, is the virtual explosion of websites offering students the opportunity to buy term papers, or even download them for free. Often presenting themselves as sources of "research assistance," these sites afford countless possibilities for plagiarism under the guise of providing "help" to students who are "in a hurry," "under pressure," or "working on a deadline." Many of these websites bury in the "FAQs" (Frequently asked questions) or "About Us" links the caveat that students should use the website's papers only as "models" for their own papers. They are, of course, quite right to include this warning. However, before you decide to use the "research assistance" these websites claim to provide, consider the criteria for evaluating Internet sites provided in Chapter 2 (see 2b-3).

In determining the usefulness of an Internet site, you should always ask about the author's credentials; for many of these "paper mill" sites, the author of the paper is anonymous and may even be another student. Why, then, should you trust the information the paper provides? Similarly, the website's URL should cause you to hesitate; paper mills typically have a ".com" address, rather than the more trustworthy ".edu" or ".gov" suffix that you might expect from a true academic site. You should also consider whether you would really want to list the site in your bibliography; it is not very likely that your professor will be impressed with a bibliographic entry for "schoolisrotten.com."

Finally, if you are ever tempted, you should also realize that if you found the website, the chances are good that your professor can find it too. It is not very hard — indeed, it is quite simple — for a professor to track down the source of a plagiarized paper.

NOTE: Ignorance about what constitutes plagiarism is not usually considered an acceptable excuse by college professors, school judicial associations, or university administrators. Read your school's policy on plagiarism and make sure you understand it. Finally, if you have any doubts or need clarification, ask your professors or consult a reference librarian.

7

Quoting and Documenting Sources

Any history paper you write reflects your careful reading and analysis of primary and secondary sources. This section offers general guidance on incorporating source material into your writing through quotation. It also explains the conventions historians use to cite and document sources.

7a. Using quotations

Quotations are an important part of writing in history. Quotations from primary sources provide evidence and support for your thesis. Quotations from secondary sources tell your readers that you are well informed about the current state of research on the issue that you are examining. The guidelines that follow will help you to decide when to quote and how to use quotations effectively.

7a-1. When to quote

Some students go to extremes, producing papers that are little more than a series of quotations loosely strung together. No matter how interesting and accurate the quotations, such a paper is no substitute for your own analysis and discussion of sources. In general, you should minimize your use of quotations, and you should choose the quotations you do use with great care.

When deciding if you should use a quotation, consider the following points.

DO·NOT QUOTE IF YOU CAN PARAPHRASE. Summarizing or paraphrasing in your own words is usually preferable to direct quotation; it demonstrates that you have digested the information from the source and made it your own. In particular, you should not quote directly if the quotation would provide only factual information. Examine this passage from *Slave Counterpoint,* a study of eighteenth-century African American culture:

ORIGINAL PASSAGE

Working alongside black women in the fields were boys and girls. Although the age at which a child entered the labor force varied from plantation to plantation, most masters in both Chesapeake and Lowcountry regarded the years of nine or ten as marking this threshold. . . . Black children, unlike their enslaved mothers, do not seem to have been singled out for any more onerous duties than their white counterparts. Those white children who left home to become servants in husbandry in early modern England generally did so at age thirteen to fourteen. However, they had probably been working for neighboring farmers on a nonresident basis from as young as seven.[1]

This passage contains a number of interesting facts. However, while it is clear and well written, there is nothing particularly significant about the wording of the passage *per se;* there are no striking analogies or turns of phrase that are particularly memorable. The paraphrase that follows includes the important facts from the original, but puts them in the writer's own words:

PARAPHRASE

Slave children began to work in the fields with their mothers at around the age of nine or ten. Their experiences as child laborers were similar to those of white children who worked in rural settings in England, where children as young as seven were sent to work on nearby farms, and moved into the homes of their employers in their early teens.

Because the original passage is merely factual, the paraphrase would be preferable to a direct quotation. The author of the paraphrase should, of course, include a footnote to indicate the source of the information. (For additional information on paraphrasing, see 6b-2.)

1. Philip D. Morgan, *Slave Counterpoint: Black Culture in the Eighteenth-Century Chesapeake and Lowcountry* (Chapel Hill: University of North Carolina Press, 1998), 197.

DO QUOTE IF THE WORDS OF THE ORIGINAL ARE ESPE-
CIALLY MEMORABLE. You might want to quote directly
when your source says something in a particularly striking
way. In the following passage, Karen Lindsey is describing
a key moment in the history of Anne Boleyn, the second
wife of King Henry VIII of England. Henry VIII had divorced his first wife, Catherine of Aragon, to marry Anne,
who, he hoped, would provide him with a son. By January 1536, Anne had produced a daughter (the future
Queen Elizabeth I) and was once again pregnant.

ORIGINAL PASSAGE

On January 29, Catherine of Aragon was buried. On the
same day Ann Boleyn, in the chilling phrase of her daughter's biographer, J. E. Neale, "miscarried of her saviour."[2]

The quotation from Neale is memorable because of the
imagery he uses to describe Anne's miscarriage, which
could not be duplicated in a summary or paraphrase.
Lindsey, then, chose an effective quotation.

You might also wish to quote when the original words
are important to readers' understanding of the author's
intentions or feelings. In the following passage from
Plato's *Apology*, Socrates is addressing the jurors who have
just condemned him to death:

ORIGINAL PASSAGE

This much I ask from you: [W]hen my sons grow up, avenge
yourselves by causing them the same kind of grief that I
caused you. . . . Reproach them as I reproach you, that they
do not care for the right things and think they are worthy
when they are not worthy of anything. If you do this, I shall
have been justly treated by you, and my sons also.[3]

In this passage, the tone is as important as the content. It
would be impossible to capture in a summary or paraphrase the irony of the original.

7a-2. How to quote

When you quote, you must follow the conventions for using
quotation marks and integrating quotations in the text of
your paper. Keep in mind the following important points.

---

2. Karen Lindsey, *Divorced, Beheaded, Survived: A Feminist Reinter-
pretation of the Wives of Henry VIII* (Reading, Mass.: Perseus Books,
1995), 115.
3. Plato, *Apology, in Five Dialogues*, trans. G. M. A. Grube (Indi-
anapolis: Hackett, 1981), 44.

INDICATE WHERE YOUR QUOTATION BEGINS AND ENDS. If you quote a source, you should quote the source's words *exactly,* and you should enclose the material from your source in quotation marks. If your quotation is more than four typed lines, you should set the quotation off by indenting it; this is called a *block quotation.* (The quotation from Socrates in 7a-1 is an example of a block quotation.) Block quotations are *not* enclosed in quotation marks. Typically, long quotations are preceded by an introductory sentence followed by a colon. You should use block quotations sparingly, if at all. Frequent use of long quotations suggests that you have not really understood the material well enough to paraphrase. Moreover, a long quotation can be distracting and cause readers to lose the thread of your argument. Use a lengthy quotation only if you have a compelling reason to do so.

KEEP QUOTATIONS BRIEF. To keep quoted material to a minimum, you should condense quoted passages by using the ellipsis mark (three periods, with spaces between), which indicates that you have left out some of the original material. If you are leaving out material at the end of a sentence, the ellipsis should be followed by a period (that is, there will be *four* periods). The quotation from Plato's *Apology* in 7a-1 contains an example of this method.

FRAME YOUR QUOTATION. Quotations from sources cannot simply be dropped into your paper. Even if a quotation is appropriate to a point you are making, you cannot assume that its significance is immediately obvious to your readers. You should always make it clear to your readers how the quotation you have chosen supports your argument. This example is from a student paper on Judge Benjamin Lindsey, the founder of the first juvenile court in the United States:

> **INEFFECTIVE**
>
> Like most progressives, Lindsey was interested in social reform. "I found no 'problem of the children' that was not also the problem of their parents."[4]

It is not clear how the quotation illustrates the writer's statement that Lindsey was interested in social reform. Are readers meant to assume that Lindsey wanted to re-

---

4. Benjamin Barr Lindsey, *The Beast* (New York: Doubleday, 1910), 151.

move children from the homes of unfit parents? Provide
government support for indigent parents? Encourage
state-funded family counseling?

In the revised version, the student frames the quotation in a way that makes its significance clear:

EFFECTIVE

> Noting that youthful offenders were often the product of
> criminal environments, Lindsey argued that even the
> most vigorous attempts to curb juvenile delinquency
> would fail until more sweeping social reforms eliminated
> the economic and social factors that led their parents to
> engage in illegal activities. Addressing the need to rehabil-
> itate and reeducate adult criminals, he wrote: "I found no
> 'problem of the children' that was not also the problem of
> their parents." Thus, for Lindsey, the reform of the juve-
> nile justice system was intrinsically linked to the reform of
> adult criminal courts.

In this revision, the significance of the quotation as it
pertains to the writer's argument is clear. The writer's
analysis before and after the quotation puts Lindsey's
words in context.

7b. Documenting sources

For all of the sources in your paper, including visual and
other nonwritten materials, you must provide complete
bibliographic information. This is important for two reasons. First, it gives appropriate credit to your sources. In
addition, bibliographic information enables readers to
look up your sources to evaluate your interpretation of
them or to read more extensively from them.

7b-1. Footnotes and endnotes

Historians typically use footnotes or endnotes to document their sources. With this method, you place a raised
number, called a *superscript*, at the end of the last word of
a quotation, paraphrase, or summary. This number corres-
ponds to a numbered note that provides bibliographic
information about your source. Notes may be placed at
the bottom of the page (footnotes) or at the end of the
paper (endnotes). In either case, notes should be numbered consecutively from the beginning to the end of the
paper.

The following example shows a source cited in the text of a paper and documented in a footnote or endnote:

TEXT

Norton argues that "the witchcraft crisis of 1692 can be comprehended only in the context of nearly two decades of armed conflict between English settlers and the New England Indians. . . ."[5]

NOTE

5. Mary Beth Norton, *In the Devil's Snare: The Salem Witchcraft Crisis of 1692* (New York: Alfred A. Knopf, 2002), 12.

You should ask your instructor if he or she has a preference for footnotes or endnotes. If the choice is left up to you, weigh the advantages and disadvantages of each form. Footnotes allow your readers to refer easily and quickly to the sources cited on a given page, but they can be distracting. Further, historians often use explanatory or discursive notes, which contain more than simple bibliographic information. (For an example of a discursive footnote, see footnote 3 from the sample paragraph on page 103.) If your paper has a large number of such footnotes in addition to bibliographic footnotes, the pages might look overwhelmed with notes. If you use endnotes, you do not need to worry about the length of your notes. However, endnotes are less accessible, requiring readers to turn to the end of the paper to refer to each note.

7b-2. Bibliography

Papers with footnotes or endnotes also need to have a bibliography — a list of all the sources consulted or cited in the paper, arranged alphabetically by authors' last names (or by title where there is no author). In a paper with endnotes, the bibliography always follows the last endnote page. (See p. 137 for a sample bibliography.)

NOTE: An alternative form of documentation that is commonly used in professional journals in the social sciences is the author-date system. The author's last name and the publication date of a cited source are included in parentheses in the text itself; complete bibliographic information appears in a reference list at the end of the text. This form of documentation is not often used in history because the author-date system is generally not practical for documenting many of the primary sources historians use. Occasionally, a history professor may suggest the use of the author-date system for a book review or for a paper citing only one or two sources, but you should not use it unless you are specifically told to do so.

7b-3. Documenting Internet sources

The Internet is an increasingly important tool for historical research. It is essential that you provide your reader with enough information to locate and examine the material you have obtained from the Internet. Documentation models for Internet and other electronic sources can be found in this manual on pages 117–20 and 130–33.

7b-4. Documenting nonwritten materials

Maps, graphs, photographs, cartoons, and other nonwritten materials can be useful in a history paper. It is not enough, however, to add these materials to your paper without discussion or explanation. When they appear in the body of a paper, visual materials, like quotations, should be incorporated into the text. Each image should include a caption that identifies it, and the text accompanying any visual material should explain its significance and its relationship to the topic of discussion. If you group visual materials in an appendix to your paper, you will also need to supply captions that identify the materials and their sources. Of course, using maps, photographs, and other nonwritten materials without full citations constitutes plagiarism. Like any other source, nonwritten materials must be cited in the bibliography.

7c. Using quotations and documenting sources: An example

A well-written history paper incorporates and documents source material. In the following paragraph, the writer has further revised the paragraph shown on pages 57–58 to include short quotations, block quotations, citations of both primary and secondary sources, and a discursive footnote:

The Chinese of the Ming dynasty were generally "uninterested in, and at times hostile to, things foreign."[1] The comments of one Ming official, Chang Han, reflect the attitude of many of his contemporaries:

> Foreigners are recalcitrant and their greed knows no bounds. . . . What is more, the greedy heart is unpredictable. If one day they break the treaties and invade our frontiers, who will be able to defend us against them?[2]

Despite this distrust, Jesuit missionaries were able to achieve positions of honor and trust in the imperial court, ultimately serving the emperor as scholars and advisers. It seems clear that the Jesuits' success in establishing cordial relations with the Chinese court was due to their initial willingness to accommodate themselves to Chinese culture. For example, realizing the extent to which the Chinese distrusted foreigners, one of the most successful of the early Jesuit missionaries, Matteo Ricci, steeped himself in Chinese culture and became fluent in Mandarin. Recognizing the importance of converting the highly educated members of the court,[3] Ricci adopted the robes of a Chinese scholar.[4] Moreover, he emphasized the similarities between Christianity and Chinese tradition, presenting Christianity as "a system of wisdom and ethics compatible with Confucianism."[5] Because of their willingness to adapt to Chinese culture, Jesuit missionaries were accepted by the imperial court until the eighteenth century. Difficulties arose, however, when the papacy forbade Chinese Christians to engage in many traditional customs, including any form of ancestor worship.[6] As the church became less accommodating to Chinese culture, relations between China and Europe deteriorated.

1. John K. Fairbank and Edwin O. Reischauer, *China: Tradition and Transformation,* rev. ed. (Boston: Houghton Mifflin, 1989), 179.

2. Chang Han, "Essay on Merchants," trans. Lily Hwa, in *Chinese Civilization and Society: A Sourcebook,* ed. Patricia Buckley Ebrey (New York: Free Press, 1981), 157.

3. The conversion of highly placed and influential officials, whose decisions might lead to conversions not only within their own households but within court circles, was an important goal for many early missionaries. For a discussion of important converts to Christianity among educated Chinese, see Jacques Gernet, *A History of Chinese Civilization,* trans. J. R. Foster and Charles Hartman, 2nd ed. (Cambridge: Cambridge University Press, 1996), 456–58.

4. Gernet, 450.

5. Fairbank and Reischauer, 245.

6. Gernet, 519; Fairbank and Reischauer, 249.

7d. Documentation models

The following models of notes and bibliographic entries illustrate the types of sources commonly used in history. The models follow *The Chicago Manual of Style,* 15th ed. (Chicago: University of Chicago Press, 2003), which is the documentation format usually preferred by historians. Your professor will probably tell you which style guide to use. (Many instructors ask their students to use Kate L. Turabian's *A Manual for Writers,* which follows *The Chicago Manual.*) Whatever style you use, be consistent: If your first footnote or endnote follows the *Chicago Manual* form, all of your notes and your bibliography should follow the *Chicago Manual.*

Notes and bibliographies follow different forms. The following example, which models a note and a bibliography entry for the same book, illustrates the differences in these two forms.

NOTE

    1. Elizabeth A. Fenn, *Pox Americana: The Great Smallpox Epidemic of 1775–82* (New York: Hill and Wang, 2001), 115.

BIBLIOGRAPHY

Fenn, Elizabeth A. *Pox Americana: The Great Smallpox Epidemic of 1775–82.* New York: Hill and Wang, 2001.

As you compare these two models, you will notice several differences:

- The note begins with an indentation and is numbered, while the first line of the bibliographic entry begins at the far left, and subsequent lines are indented.
- In the note form, the author's name appears in the conventional order (first name, middle initial, last name), while the bibliography lists authors by their last names; the first name and initials are separated from the last name by a comma.
- Commas separate the author and title in the note, while the author's name and the title are followed by periods in the bibliography.
- In the note form, the place of publication, the publisher, and the date are enclosed in parentheses; in the bibliography, no parentheses are used.

- The note refers the reader to the specific pages being cited; the bibliography cites the book.

Models for notes are given on pages 106 to 120. Bibliographic entries for the same sources are given on pages 120 to 133 and are distinguished by the darker side band.

7d-1. Models for footnotes and endnotes

Books

A typical note for a book includes the following information:

- The author's full name (or the editor's full name, if no author is listed), followed by a comma;
- The full title of the book, italicized;
- Publication information: the city of publication, followed by a colon (if more than one city is listed, you need only include the first; no state is needed for well-known cities); the name of the publisher, followed by a comma ("Inc.," "Co.," and other abbreviations are not needed); and the date of publication — all enclosed in parentheses and followed by a comma;
- The page or pages cited, followed by a period.

Individual entries should be single-spaced; double-space between notes. Typically, the first line of each note is indented.

BASIC FORM FOR A BOOK

1. Robert McGhee, *The Last Imaginary Place: A Human History of the Arctic World* (Oxford: Oxford University Press, 2005), 197.

SHORTENED FORMS IN SUBSEQUENT REFERENCES

The first time you cite a work, you must provide complete bibliographic information. In subsequent references, however, use a shortened form. There are two acceptable methods to shorten a reference. In one, you can cite the author's last name followed by a comma and the page or pages cited.

> 2. McGhee, 232.

In the second, you may also include a shortened form of the title in your subsequent reference. This is necessary if you cite more than one work by the same author in your paper or if a subsequent reference appears long after the first reference. To shorten the title, use the key word or words from the title of the book or article.

> 3. McGhee, *Last Imaginary Place,* 46.

ABBREVIATIONS IN SUBSEQUENT REFERENCES

Ibid. The abbreviation "ibid." (from the Latin *ibidem,* meaning "in the same place") is sometimes used to refer to the work cited in the previous note. However, many professors and professional journals prefer the author/page or the author/short title/page style. Be sure you know which method your professor prefers.

When it is used, "ibid." stands in place of both the author's name and the title of the work. If you are referring to the same page, use "ibid." alone; if you are referring to different page numbers, use "ibid." followed by a comma and the new page numbers.

> 4. Ibid., 79-84.

NOTE: Never use "ibid." if the previous note refers to more than one work.

TWO OR MORE AUTHORS

If a book has two or more authors, list the authors in your note in the order in which their names appear on the title page.

> 5. Philip F. Williams and Yenna Wu, *The Great Wall of Confinement: The Chinese Prison Camp Through Contemporary Fiction and Reportage* (Berkeley: University of California Press, 2004), 153.

NOTE: For books with more than three authors, you may use the Latin term "et al." ("and others") after the first author instead of listing all the authors (for example, "Jane Doe et al.").

AUTHOR'S NAME IN THE TITLE

Sometimes an author's name appears in the title of a book, as in an autobiography or a collection of letters or papers. In this case, your footnote or endnote should begin with the title of the book.

6. *Charles Darwin's Letters: A Selection, 1825-1859,* ed. Frederick Burkhardt (Cambridge: Cambridge University Press, 1996), 15-19.

ANONYMOUS WORK

If the author of a work is unknown and if there is no editor or compiler, begin your note with the title.

7. *DK Atlas of World History* (New York: Dorling Kindersley, 2000), 33.

EDITED OR COMPILED WORK WITHOUT AN AUTHOR

Cite a book by its editor (abbreviated "ed.") or compiler (abbreviated "comp.") if no author appears on the title page (as in a collection or anthology).

8. M. Mohamed Salih, ed., *African Parliament: Between Governments and Governance* (New York: Palgrave Macmillan, 2005), 59-60.

EDITED WORK WITH AN AUTHOR

If an author's name is provided in addition to an editor's, give the editor's name after the title.

9. Efraim Karsh, *Empires of the Sand: The Struggle for Mastery in the Middle East, 1789-1923,* ed. Inari Karsh (Cambridge, MA: Harvard University Press, 1999), 303-04.

A book with multiple editors should be treated the same way as a book with multiple authors; list the editors in the order in which they appear on the title page.

10. Robert M. Levine and John L. Crocitti, eds., *The Brazil Reader: History, Culture, Politics* (Durham: Duke University Press, 1999), 436.

TRANSLATED WORK

A translator's name, like an editor's, is placed after the title when an author's name is given. If a source has an editor and a translator, then both should be listed.

11. Xie Bingying, *A Woman Soldier's Own Story,* trans. Barry Brissman and Lily Chia Brissman (New York: Columbia University Press, 2001), 296.

12. Roman Vishniac, *Children of a Vanished World,* S. Mark Taper Foundation Book in Jewish Studies, ed. Mara Vishniac Kohn, trans. Miriam Hartman Flacks (Berkeley: University of California Press, 1999), 23.

MULTIVOLUME WORK

If an individual volume of a multivolume work does not have its own title, include the volume number and the page numbers after the publication information.

13. Bonnie S. Anderson and Judith P. Zinsser, *A Place of Their Own: Women in Europe from Prehistory to the Present,* rev. ed. (New York: Oxford University Press, 2000), 2: 172-73.

If a single volume in a multivolume work has a separate title, include the volume number and title directly after the general title:

14. Hermann Kinder and Werner Hilgemann, *The Penguin Atlas of World History,* vol. 1, *From Prehistory to the Eve of the French Revolution,* rev. ed. (New York: Penguin Books, 2004), 176.

DOCUMENT OR ARTICLE IN A COLLECTION OR ANTHOLOGY

If you cite a document or article from a collection or anthology, include the author and title of the document or article, followed by the title, editor, and publication information for the book in which it appears. Also give the page or pages on which the information you are citing appears.

15. Thomas Paine, *Common Sense,* in *Our Nation's Archive: The History of the United States in Documents,* ed. Erik Bruun and Jay Crosby (New York: Black Dog and Leventhal, 1999), 124.

CHAPTER IN AN EDITED WORK

When you are citing a book that has an editor or multiple editors, but in which the chapters have individual authors, you should cite the author and title of the chapter first, followed by the title, editor, and publication information for the book.

16. Bernard Hamilton, "The Impact of the Crusades on Western Geographical Knowledge," in *Eastward Bound: Travel and Travellers, 1050-1550,* ed. Rosamund Allen (Manchester: Manchester University Press, 2004), 17-18.

LETTER IN A PUBLISHED COLLECTION

When citing a letter that appears in a published collection, list the sender, recipient, and date of the communication, and then cite the collection as you would a book.

17. An Expectant Mother to Eleanor Roosevelt, January 2, 1935, *America 1900-1999: Letters of the Century*, ed. Lisa Grunwald and Stephen J. Adler (New York: Dial Press, 1999), 223.

EDITION OTHER THAN THE FIRST

If the text you are using is not the first edition, provide the edition number in your note.

18. Chafe, William H., *The Unfinished Journey: America since World War II,* 5th ed. (New York: Oxford University Press, 2002), 247.

WORK IN A SERIES

Some books are part of a series: publications on the same general subject that are supervised by a general editor or group of editors. The series title and series editor may be eliminated from your note if the book can be located easily without them.

19. Brett Flehinger, *The 1912 Election and the Power of Progressivism: A Brief History with Documents,* Bedford Series in History and Culture (Boston: Bedford/St. Martin's, 2003), 147-48.

Periodicals

A typical note for an article in a journal includes the following information:

- The author's full name, followed by a comma;
- The title of the article, in quotation marks and followed by a comma;

- The name of the journal in which the article appears, italicized;
- The volume number (in arabic numerals, even if the journal uses roman numerals);
- The date, in parentheses, followed by a colon;
- The page or pages cited, followed by a period.

ARTICLE IN A JOURNAL PAGINATED BY VOLUME

Most scholarly journals are paginated consecutively throughout the volume. When citing an article from such a journal, you do not need to give the issue number, although this information may be useful, especially for recent, unbound journals.

20. Lisa Lucero, "The Collapse of the Classic Maya: A Case for the Role of Water Control," *American Anthropologist* 104 (2002): 817-18.

ARTICLE IN A JOURNAL PAGINATED BY ISSUE

If a journal paginates each issue separately, you must provide the issue number. In the following model (one of several acceptable forms for citing the issue of a journal), the volume number is 283, the issue number is 5, the year of publication is 2000, and the page reference is 668.

21. Rhoda Wynn, "Saints and Sinners: Women and the Practice of Medicine throughout the Ages," *Journal of the American Medical Association* 283, no. 5 (2000): 668.

NOTE: If you wish to include the month of publication, put it before the year: (March 2000). If you include the month, you do not need the issue number.

ARTICLE IN A POPULAR MAGAZINE

In citing an article from a popular magazine, include the author, title of the article, magazine title, and date (not in parentheses). Omit the volume and issue numbers. It is not necessary to include page numbers; if you do include them, they should be preceded by a comma, not a colon.

22. Evan Thomas, "The Day That Changed America," *Newsweek Special Double Issue,* December 2001-January 2002, 45-46.

NEWSPAPER ARTICLE

When referring to an article in a daily newspaper, always cite the author's name (if it is given), the title of the article, date, month, and year. Each issue of a newspaper may go through several editions, and in each edition articles may be rearranged or even eliminated entirely. For this reason, you should cite the name of the edition in which the article appeared (for example, first edition, late edition). Page numbers are usually omitted. If you are citing a large newspaper that is published in sections, include the name, letter, or number of the section.

    23. Hamil R. Harris and Darryl Fears, "Thousands Pay Respects to King," *Washington Post,* February 5, 2006, sec. A, Maryland edition.

NOTE: If the city of the newspaper is not well known, include the state in parentheses.

BOOK REVIEW

To cite a book review, begin with the reviewer's name followed by the title of the review, if one is given. Follow this information by the words "review of," the title of the work being reviewed, and its author. Also cite the periodical in which the review appears and the relevant publication information. If the author of the review is not named, begin with the title of the review or, if the review is untitled, with the words "Review of."

    24. Ilene Cooper, review of *Nat Turner's Slave Rebellion in American History,* by Judith Edwards, *Booklist* 96 (2000): 1093.

    25. Review of *A Middle East Mosaic: Fragments of Life, Letters, and History,* by Bernard Lewis, ed., *Publishers Weekly,* March 24, 2000, 80.

Public documents

In the United States, most federal government publications are printed by the Government Printing Office in Washington, D.C., and may be issued by both houses of Congress (the House of Representatives and the Senate); by the executive departments (for example, the Department of State, the Department of the Interior, and so on); or by government commissions or agencies (for example, the Securities and Exchange Commission). In addition, public documents may be issued by state or local governments. A reference to a public document should include the following:

- The name of the country, state, city, or county from which the document was issued (papers on United States history may omit "United States" or "U.S.");
- The name of the legislative body, court, executive department, or other agency issuing the document;
- The title of the document or collection, if given;
- The name of the author, editor, or compiler;
- The report number;
- The publisher, if applicable ("Government Printing Office" may be shortened to "GPO");
- The date;
- The page or pages cited.

The following models are for notes citing government documents commonly used by students writing history papers.

PRESIDENTIAL PAPERS

The Government Printing Office has published the papers of the presidents of the United States in two multivolume collections: *Compilation of the Messages and Papers of the Presidents, 1789–1897* for the early presidency and *Public Papers of the Presidents of the United States* for twentieth-century presidents.

26. Dwight D. Eisenhower, *Public Papers of the Presidents of the United States: Dwight D. Eisenhower,* 1953 (Washington, DC: GPO, 1960), 228-30.

For the presidencies of George Herbert Walker Bush, William Jefferson Clinton, and George W. Bush (January 1992–June 2001), *Public Papers for the President of the United States* are available online at www.gpoaccess.gov/multidb.html.

EXECUTIVE DEPARTMENT DOCUMENT

A note for a document issued by one of the executive departments begins with the issuing department. Include the name of the author of the document, if it is known. If the publication is part of a series, you may include the series number and omit the publication information.

27. U.S. General Accounting Office, *Desert Shield and Desert Storm Reports and Testimonies, 1991-93* (Washington, DC: General Accounting Office, 1994), 446.

28. U.S. Department of State, *Belarus,* Background Notes Series, no. 10344, 77.

TESTIMONY BEFORE A COMMITTEE

Transcripts of testimony presented before congressional committees or commissions can be found in records called "hearings." Begin the note with the committee or commission name.

29. Senate Committee on Homeland Security and Governmental Affairs, *Chemical Attack on America: How Vulnerable Are We? Hearing before the Committee on Homeland Security and Governmental Affairs,* 109th Cong., 1st sess., 2005, 71-72.

CONGRESSIONAL COMMITTEE PRINT

Both houses of Congress issue research reports called "Committee Prints." Your note should include either the date or the Committee Print number, if one is provided.

30. U.S. Congress, House Committee on Ways and Means, *Report on Trade Mission to Colombia, Ecuador, and Peru,* 109th Cong., 1st sess., 2005, Committee Print, 109-6, 15.

TREATY

Treaties can be found in volumes of *United States Treaties and Other International Agreements,* issued by the Government Printing Office. Each treaty in the bound volume was originally published in pamphlet form in a State Department series titled Treaties and Other International Acts (TIAS). In your note, the title (in quotation marks) and date of a treaty should follow the name of the issuing agency (such as U.S. Department of State). The number assigned to the treaty in TIAS is given in the bound volume and should also be included in your note.

31. U.S. Department of State, "Jay Treaty," November 19, 1794, TIAS no. 105, *United States Treaties and Other International Agreements,* vol. 2, 245.

UNITED STATES CONSTITUTION

The Constitution is cited by article (abbreviated "art.") or amendment ("amend.") and section ("sec.").

32. U.S. Constitution, art. 4, sec. 1.

The forms of notes for state and local government publications are the same as those for federal government publications.

Other sources

UNPUBLISHED THESIS OR DISSERTATION

To cite an unpublished thesis or dissertation, give its author, title (in quotation marks), academic institution, and date.

33. J. W. Lee, "Paul and the Politics of Difference: A Contextual Study of Jewish-Gentile Difference in Galatians and Romans" (PhD diss., Union Theological Seminary, 2002), 67.

UNPUBLISHED LETTER IN A MANUSCRIPT COLLECTION

When citing material from manuscript collections, begin with the specific item, followed by its location. For a letter, start with the name of the letter writer, followed by the name of the recipient and the date. Full identifying information about the collection in which the letter is found should follow, beginning with the file, box or container number, if known; the name of the collection; and its location.

34. Nathaniel Hawthorne to James W. Beekman, April 9, 1853, letter box 3, "James W. Beekman Papers," New-York Historical Society, New York.

ILLUSTRATION, TABLE, OR MAP

In citing an illustration, table, or map in a printed text, give both the page number on which the illustration appears and the figure or plate number, if one is provided.

35. Owen Gingerich, *The Book Nobody Read: Chasing the Revolutions of Nicolaus Copernicus* (New York: Walker, 2004), 153.

36. William Lewis Herndon, *Exploration of the Valley of the Amazon, 1851-1852,* ed. Gary Kinder (New York: Grove Press, 2000), 85, Plate 9.

SOUND RECORDING

Notes for sound recordings, including audiotapes, compact discs, and records, begin with the composer's name followed by the title of the recording (italicized or underlined) and the name of the performer. Also provide the name of the recording company and the number.

37. Gustav Holst, *The Planets,* Royal Philharmonic Orchestra, André Previn, Telarc compact disc 80133.

For an anonymous work or a collection of works by several composers, begin with the title.

38. *Virtuoso Recorder Music*, Amsterdam Loeki Stardust Quartet, Decca compact disc 414 277-2.

FILM, VIDEOCASSETTE, OR DVD

A note for a film, videocassette, or DVD should include the title of the episode (if part of a series), the title of the film, the name of the producer and director, the playing time, the name of the production company, and the date. Videocassettes and DVDs should be identified as such.

39. "Forever Free," *The Civil War*, produced by Ken Burns, 76 minutes, PBS Video, 1990, videocassette.

INTERVIEW

A note for an interview that has been published or broadcast on radio or television should include the name of the person interviewed, the title of the interview (if any), the name of the person who conducted the interview, the medium in which the interview appeared (radio, television, book, journal), and the facts of publication.

40. President George W. Bush, interviewed by Bob Schieffer, *Face the Nation*, CBS, January 27, 2006.

PERSONAL COMMUNICATION

A note for an interview you have conducted in person or by telephone should include the name of the person you interviewed, the words "interview by author," the place of the interview, if applicable, and the interview date.

41. Michael Coleman, telephone interview by author, March 23, 2006.

A personal letter or memorandum to you should be cited in the same way as a personal interview.

42. Audrey Hamilton, letter to author, August 21, 2005.

REFERENCE WORK

In a note for a standard reference work that is arranged alphabetically, such as a dictionary or an encyclopedia, omit the publication information, as well as the volume and page references. You must, however, note the edition if it is not the first. After the name and edition of the work, use the abbreviation "s.v." (for *sub verbo*, "under the word") followed by the title of the entry in quotation marks.

43. *Encyclopaedia Britannica,* 15th ed. rev., s.v. "steam power."

44. *Merriam-Webster's Collegiate Dictionary,* 11th ed., s.v. "civilization."

BIBLICAL REFERENCE

When referring to a passage from the Bible, cite the book (abbreviated), chapter, and verse, either in the text or in a note. Do not provide a page number. In your first biblical reference, identify the version of the Bible you are using; in subsequent references, abbreviate the version.

45. Matt. 20.4-9 Revised Standard Version.

46. 1 Chron. 4.13-15 RSV.

Chapters and verses in biblical references have traditionally been separated by a colon, but in current usage they are separated by a period.

INDIRECT SOURCE

If material you wish to use from a source has been taken from another source, it is always preferable to find and consult the original source. If this is not possible, you must acknowledge both the original source of the material and your own source for the information.

47. E. W. Creak, "On the Mariner's Compass in Modern Vessels of War," *Journal of the Royal United Services Institute,* vol. 33 (1889-90), 966, quoted in Alan Gurney, *Compass: A Story of Exploration and Innovation* (New York: Norton, 2004), 275-76.

Electronic sources

To cite a document or other material that is available on the World Wide Web, you should include as much of the following material as possible: the author's name, if known; the title of the document or Web page; the title or owner of the site; and the URL. Include the date on which the site was accessed if it is likely to have frequent substantive updates or the material is particularly time sensitive. When access dates are given, they should be enclosed in parentheses: (accessed July 23, 2005).

WHOLE WEBSITE WITH A KNOWN AUTHOR

If you wish to cite a complete website, include the author's name, the title of the website italicized, and the URL.

48. E. L. Skip Knox, *The Crusades,* http://crusades .boisestate.edu.

WHOLE WEBSITE WITH AN UNKNOWN AUTHOR

If you are citing a website whose authorship is unknown, begin with the owner of the site:

51. The Ohio State Department of History, "The Scopes Trial," http://history.osu.edu/Projects/Clash/Scopes/ scopes-page1.htm.

SELECTION FROM A WEBSITE

To cite a selection from a website, list the author (if known); the title of the selection, in quotation marks; the title of the site, italicized; and the URL.

50. Douglas Linder, "An Account of Events in Salem," *Famous Trials,* www.law.umkc.edu/faculty/projects/ftrials/salem/ sal_acct.htm.

ONLINE BOOK

A citation for an online book should include the following information: the author of the book; the title of the book, italicized; the place and date of publication (if known), in parentheses; the project title and date; and the URL. Include the date on which the site was accessed, in parentheses, if the material is time sensitive.

51. Alfred Russell Wallace, *The Malay Archipelago* (1869), Project Gutenberg, February 2001, ftp://ibiblio.org/pub/docs/ books/gutenberg/etext01/1malay10.txt.

If you have accessed an online book through an authored website, your note should also include the author, name, and date of the website, if known.

52. Cotton Mather, *Memorable Providences, Relating to Witch-crafts and Possessions* (Boston: 1689), at Douglas Linder, *Famous Trials,* www.law.umkc.edu/faculty/projects/ftrials/salem/ asa_math.htm.

ARTICLE IN AN ELECTRONIC JOURNAL

A citation for an article in an electronic journal should include the author's name; the title of the article, in quotation marks; the title of the journal, italicized; the number of the journal; the date of publication, in parentheses; the URL; and the date of access, in parentheses, if the material is time sensitive.

53. Shamma Friedman, "A Good Story Deserves Retelling--The Unfolding of the Akiva Legend," *Jewish Studies: An Internet Journal* 3 (2004), www.biu.ac.il/JS/JSIJ/3-2004/Friedman.pdf.

ARTICLE ACCESSED THROUGH AN ELECTRONIC DATABASE

To cite an article from a print journal accessed through an electronic database, add the following to the information you would include for a journal article in print: the name of the online database; the URL for the database, and the date of access, in parentheses, if the material is time sensitive.

54. Robert Brent Toplin, "The Filmmaker as Historian," *American Historical Review* 93 (1988): 1210–27. *JSTOR,* www .jstor.org.

ONLINE GOVERNMENT PUBLICATION

A citation for a government publication should include the author; the title of the document; the type of document; the date of publication; the URL; and the date of access, in parentheses, if the material is time sensitive.

55. George W. Bush, "Improving Agency Disclosure of Information," Executive Order, December 14, 2005, www.whitehouse .gov/news/releases/2005/12/20051214-4.html (accessed January 3, 2006).

ONLINE NEWSPAPER ARTICLE

To cite an online newspaper article, include the author, if known; the title of the article; the name of the newspaper; the date of publication; the URL; and the date of access, in parentheses, if the material is time sensitive.

56. Dafna Linzer, "Strong Leads and Dead Ends in Nuclear Case Against Iran," *Washington Post.com,* February 8, 2006, www.washingtonpost.com/wp-dyn/content/article/2006/02/ 07/AR2006020702126.html (accessed February 9, 2006).

ONLINE REVIEW

A citation for an online review should include the name of the reviewer; the title and author of the book being reviewed; the name of the online publication; the date of the review; the URL; and the date of access, in parentheses, if the material is time sensitive.

57. Anthony Lewis, review of *At Canaan's Edge: America in the King Years, 1965-68,* by Taylor Branch, *New York Times,* February 5, 2006, www.nytimes.com/2006/02/05/books/review/ 05lewis.html (accessed February 10, 2006).

WEB FORUM, LISTSERV, OR NEWSGROUP POSTING

To document a posting to a Web discussion forum, listserv, or newsgroup, include the author's name; the title of the posting, in quotation marks; the name of the list; the date of the posting; the URL; and the date of access, in parentheses, if the material is time sensitive.

58. Lowell W. Gudmundson, "INFO: New On-Line Materials on Afro-Central Amrican History," e-mail to H-Net Latin American History forum, February 3, 2006, http://h-net.msu.edu/cgi -bin/logbrowse.pl?trx=vx&list=H-LatAm&month=0602 (accessed February 8, 2006).

E-MAIL MESSAGE

Include the author's name; the type of communication; the date of the posting; and the date of access.

59. Kathy Retan, e-mail message to author, May 10, 2005.

NOTE: You should never include personal e-mail addresses in your citations.

CD-ROM

Materials published on CD-ROM should be documented in the same way as printed works.

60. Naomi Reed Kline, *A Wheel of Memory: The Hereford Mappamundi,* CD-ROM (Ann Arbor: University of Michigan Press, 2001).

7d-2. Models for bibliography entries

Your bibliography is a list of the books, articles, and other sources you used in preparing your paper. It must include all the works you cited in your notes; it may also include other works that you consulted but did not cite. However, avoid the temptation to pad your bibliography; list only materials you did in fact use.

You should list works in your bibliography alphabetically by authors' last names. If your bibliography is long, you may wish to divide it into sections. You might, for example, create separate headings such as "Primary Sources" and "Books and Articles." If you have used manuscripts or other unpublished sources, you might list these separately as well.

Books

A typical bibliography entry for a book contains the following information:

- The author's full name, last name first, followed by a period;
- The full title of the book, italicized, followed by a period;
- The city of publication, followed by a colon;
- The name of the publisher, followed by a comma;
- The date of publication, followed by a period.

Typically, the first line of a bibliography entry is typed flush left, and subsequent lines are indented. Individual entries should be single-spaced; double-space between entries.

BASIC FORM FOR A BOOK

McGhee, Robert. *The Last Imaginary Place: A Human History of the Arctic World*. Oxford: Oxford University Press, 2005.

MULTIPLE WORKS BY THE SAME AUTHOR

If your bibliography includes more than one work by the same author, you should use three dashes (or three hyphens) followed by a period (---.) in place of the author's name in subsequent bibliographic entries.

McGhee, Robert. *Ancient People of the Arctic.* Vancouver:
     University of British Columbia Press, 1996.
---. *The Last Imaginary Place: A Human History of the Arctic
     World.* Oxford University Press, 2005.

TWO OR MORE AUTHORS

An entry for a book with two or more authors should
begin with the name of the first author listed on the title
page, last name first. The names of the other authors are
given in normal order.

Williams, Philip F., and Yenna Wu. *The Great Wall of Confine-
     ment: The Chinese Prison Camp Through Contemporary
     Fiction and Reportage.* Berkeley: University of California
     Press, 2004.

AUTHOR'S NAME IN THE TITLE

Begin the bibliography entry with the author's name,
even if it appears in the title.

Darwin, Charles. *Charles Darwin's Letters: A Selection, 1825-
     1859.* Edited by Frederick Burkhardt. Cambridge: Cambridge
     University Press, 1996.

ANONYMOUS WORK

If the author of a work is unknown, list the work in the
bibliography by its title. If the title begins with an article
(*A, An,* or *The*), alphabetize the book according to the first
letter of the next word.

DK Atlas of World History. New York: Dorling Kindersley, 2000.

EDITED OR COMPILED WORK WITHOUT AN AUTHOR

List a book by the last name of the editor, translator, or
compiler if no author appears on the title page (as in a
collection or anthology).

Salih, M. Mohammed, ed. *African Parliament: Between Govern-
     ments and Governance.* New York: Palgrave Macmillan, 2005.

EDITED WORK WITH AN AUTHOR

For a book with an author as well as an editor, the editor's
name follows the title.

Karsh, Efraim. *Empires of the Sand: The Struggle for Mastery in
     the Middle East, 1789-1923.* Edited by Inari Karsh.
     Cambridge, MA: Harvard University Press, 1999.

An entry for a book with multiple editors should be treated the same way as a book with multiple authors; list the editors in the order in which they appear on the title page. The first editor's last name should be given first, with names of subsequent editors given in the normal order.

Levine, Robert M., and John L. Crocitti, eds. *The Brazil Reader: History, Culture, Politics.* Durham: Duke University Press 1999.

TRANSLATED WORK

A translator's name, like an editor's, is placed after the title when an author's name is given. If a source has an editor and a translator, both should be listed.

Bingying, Xie. *A Woman Soldier's Own Story.* Translated by Barry Brissman and Lily Chia Brissman. New York: Columbia University Press, 2001.

MULTIVOLUME WORK

For a multivolume work, include the number of volumes in the bibliography entry.

Anderson, Bonnie S., and Judith P. Zinsser. *A Place of Their Own: Women in Europe from Prehistory to the Present.* Rev. ed. 2 vols. New York: Oxford University Press, 2000.

If you have used a single volume of a multivolume set, cite only that volume.

Kinder, Hermann, and Werner Hilgemann. *The Penguin Atlas of World History.* Vol. 1, *From Prehistory to the Eve of the French Revolution.* Rev. ed. New York: Penguin Books, 2004.

DOCUMENT OR ARTICLE IN A COLLECTION OR ANTHOLOGY

List a document or article in a collection or anthology by the author of the article. You may include the pages on which the article begins and ends.

Paine, Thomas. *Common Sense.* In *Our Nation's Archive: The History of the United States in Documents,* edited by Erik Bruun and Jay Crosby, 123-27. New York: Black Dog and Leventhal, 1999.

CHAPTER IN AN EDITED WORK

When you are citing a book that has an editor or multiple editors, but in which the chapters have individual authors, you should cite the author and title of the chapter first, followed by the title, editor, and publication information for the book.

Hamilton, Bernard. "The Impact of the Crusades on Western Geographical Knowledge." In *Eastward Bound: Travel and Travellers, 1050-1550,* edited by Rosamund Allen, 15-34. Manchester: Manchester University Press, 2004.

LETTER IN A PUBLISHED COLLECTION

If you cite only one letter from a collection, you may list it as an individual letter in your bibliography.

An Expectant Mother to Eleanor Roosevelt, January 2, 1935. In *America 1900-1999: Letters of the Century,* ed. Lisa Grunwald and Stephen J. Adler. New York: Dial Press, 1999.

However, if you cite several letters from the same collection, list only the collection.

America 1900-1999: Letters of the Century. Ed. Lisa Grunwald and Stephen J. Adler. New York: Dial Press, 1999.

EDITION OTHER THAN THE FIRST

If you are using any edition other than the first, include the edition number in your bibliography.

Chafe, William H. *The Unfinished Journey: America since World War II,* 5th ed. New York: Oxford University Press, 2002.

WORK IN A SERIES

A series is a set of publications on the same general subject that is supervised by an editor or group of editors. Begin the entry with the author and title of the individual work from the series followed by the title of the series. The name of the series editor is usually omitted.

Flehinger, Brett. *The 1912 Election and the Power of Progressivism: A Brief History with Documents.* Bedford Series in History and Culture. Boston: Bedford/St. Martin's, 2003.

Periodicals

A typical bibliography entry for an article in a journal includes the following information:

- The author's full name, last name first, followed by a period;
- The title of the article, in quotation marks and followed by a period;
- The name of the journal, italicized;
- The volume number, in arabic numerals;
- The date, in parentheses, followed by a colon;
- The pages on which the article begins and ends, followed by a period.

ARTICLE IN A JOURNAL PAGINATED BY VOLUME

Most scholarly journals are paginated consecutively throughout the volume. When citing an article from such a journal, it is not mandatory that you give the issue number.

Lucero, Lisa. "The Collapse of the Classic Maya: A Case for the Role of Water Control." *American Anthropologist* 104 (2002): 814-26.

ARTICLE IN A JOURNAL PAGINATED BY ISSUE

If a journal paginates each issue separately, you must provide the issue number.

Wynn, Rhoda. "Saints and Sinners: Women and the Practice of Medicine throughout the Ages." *Journal of the American Medical Association* 283, no. 5 (2000): 668.

NOTE: If you wish to include the month of publication, put it before the year: (March 2000). If you include the month, you do not need the issue number.

ARTICLE IN A POPULAR MAGAZINE

It is not necessary to give the volume number or issue number for an article in a popular magazine. If you include page numbers, they are preceded by a comma, not by a colon.

Thomas, Evan. "The Day That Changed America." *Newsweek Special Double Issue,* December 2001-January 2002, 45-46.

NEWSPAPER ARTICLE

If you consulted various articles from a particular newspaper, you don't have to list the articles separately in the bibliography. Instead, provide just the name of the paper and the range of dates of the issues you consulted.

Washington Post, December 2005-January 2006.

BOOK REVIEW

List a book review by the reviewer's last name. If the author of the review is not named, begin with the title of the review or, if the review is untitled, with the words "Review of."

Cooper, Ilene. Review of *Nat Turner's Slave Rebellion in American History*, by Judith Edwards. *Booklist* 96 (2000): 1093.

Review of *A Middle East Mosaic: Fragments of Life, Letters, and History*, edited by Bernard Lewis. *Publishers Weekly*, March 24, 2000, 80.

Public documents

The same information should be provided as for notes (see pp. 112–14). In a paper on United States history, you may omit "United States" or "U.S." as the country in which a document was issued if it is clear in context.

PRESIDENTIAL PAPERS

Entries for these papers often begin with and are alphabetized by the president's name.

Eisenhower, Dwight D. *Public Papers of the Presidents of the United States: Dwight D. Eisenhower, 1953*. Washington, DC: GPO, 1960.

EXECUTIVE DEPARTMENT DOCUMENT

Entries for these documents begin with the issuing department's name.

U.S. General Accounting Office. *Desert Shield and Desert Storm Reports and Testimonies, 1991–93*. Washington, DC: General Accounting Office, 1994.

U.S. Department of State. *Belarus*. Background Notes Series, no. 10344.

TESTIMONY BEFORE A COMMITTEE

If you cite or consult a transcript of testimony before a committee, begin the entry with the name of the committee.

Senate Committee on Homeland Security and Government Affairs.
    Chemical Attack on America: How Vulnerable Are We?
    Hearing before the Committee on Homeland Security and
    Governmental Affairs. 109th Cong., 1st sess., 2005.

CONGRESSIONAL COMMITTEE PRINT

Entries for these research reports should include the print number or date.

U.S. Congress. House Committee on Ways and Means. *Report on*
    Trade Mission to Colombia, Ecuador, and Peru. 109th Cong.,
    1st sess., 2005. Committee Print.

TREATY

Begin the entry with the name of the issuing agency.

U.S. Department of State. "Jay Treaty," November 19, 1794. TIAS
    no. 105. *United States Treaties and Other International*
    Agreements, vol. 2.

(See p. 114 for information about the TIAS number.)

UNITED STATES CONSTITUTION

If you cite the Constitution in your paper, you *do not* need to include it in your bibliography.

Other sources

UNPUBLISHED THESIS OR DISSERTATION

List an unpublished thesis or dissertation by its author's last name.

Lee, J. W. "Paul and the Politics of Difference: A Contextual
    Study of Jewish-Gentile Difference in Galatians and Romans."
    PhD diss., Union Theological Seminary, 2002.

UNPUBLISHED LETTER IN A MANUSCRIPT COLLECTION

If you have used material from manuscript collections, the bibliography entry should begin with the specific item, followed by its location. For a letter, start with the name of the author of the collected manuscripts or the title of the collection, followed by the depository and its location.

Beekman, James W. *Papers*. New-York Historical Society, New York.

If you have only cited one item from the collection, list it under the name of the author.

Hawthorne, Nathaniel. Letter to James W. Beekman. *James W. Beekman Papers*. New-York Historical Society, New York.

ILLUSTRATION, TABLE, OR MAP

For an illustration, table, or map in a printed text, give the author, title, city, publisher, and year.

Herndon, William Lewis. *Exploration of the Valley of the Amazon, 1851-1852*. Edited by Gary Kinder. New York: Grove Press, 2000.

SOUND RECORDING

List a sound recording by the composer's last name or, for a collection or an anonymous work, by the title of the recording. Include the recording company and number if they are provided.

Holst, Gustav. *The Planets*. Royal Philharmonic Orchestra. André Previn. Telarc compact disc 80133.

Virtuoso Recorder Music. Amsterdam Loeki Stardust Quartet. Decca compact disc 414 277-2.

FILM, VIDEOCASSETTE, OR DVD

After the film title, include the name of the producer and director, the playing time, the production company, the date, and the medium.

The Civil War. Produced by Ken Burns. 11 hours. PBS Video, 1990. 9 videocassettes.

INTERVIEW

List an interview under the name of the person interviewed and provide the date of the interview.

Bush, George W. Interviewed by Bob Schieffer. *Face the Nation*, CBS, January 27, 2006.

PERSONAL COMMUNICATION

Because your reader will not have access to personal interviews you conducted or letters you received, you *do not* need to list these sources in your bibliography.

REFERENCE WORKS AND THE BIBLE

Well-known reference works and the Bible are usually not included in bibliographies.

INDIRECT SOURCE

If material you have taken from one source originally appeared in another source and you have not consulted the original yourself, your bibliography entry should begin with the original source but must include your own source for the information. The page numbers from both sources should be included.

Creak, E. W. "On the Mariner's Compass in Modern Vessels of War." *Journal of the Royal United Services Institute,* 33 (1889-90): 949-75. Quoted in Alan Gurney. *Compass: A Story of Exploration and Innovation.* New York: W. W. Norton, 2004.

Electronic sources

WHOLE WEBSITE WITH A KNOWN AUTHOR

Bibliographic entries for a complete website with a known author should begin with the author's last name. Periods, rather than commas, are used to separate the elements of the entry. Include access dates, in parentheses, if the material is time sensitive.

Knox, E. L. Skip. "The Crusades." http://crusades.boisestate.edu.

WHOLE WEBSITE WITH AN UNKNOWN AUTHOR

If you are citing a website whose authorship is unknown, begin with the owner of the website. Use periods in place of commas to separate the title, date, and URL.

The Ohio State University Department of History. "The Scopes Trial." http://history.osu.edu/Projects/Clash/Scopes/ scopes-page1.htm.

SELECTION FROM A WEB SITE

To cite a selection from a website, begin with the last name of the author of the selection (if known). Separate the elements of the citation with periods.

Linder, Douglas. "An Account of Events in Salem." *Famous Trials.*
www.law.umkc.edu/faculty/projects/ftrials/salem/
sal_acct.htm.

ONLINE BOOK

A bibliographic citation for an online book should begin
with the last name of the author of the book. If you access an online book through an authored website, also include the author, name, and date of the website, if
known.

Wallace, Alfred Russell. *The Malay Archipelago.* 1869. Project
Gutenberg. February 2001. ftp://ibiblio.org/pub/docs/
books/gutenberg/etext01/1malay10.txt.

Mather, Cotton. *Memorable Providences, Relating to Witchcrafts
and Possessions.* Boston: 1689. At Douglas Linder. *Famous
Trials.* www.law.umkc.edu/faculty/projects/ftrials/salem/
asa_math.htm.

ARTICLE IN AN ELECTRONIC JOURNAL

A citation for an article in an electronic journal should
begin with the author's last name. Elements of the entry
should be separated by periods.

Friedman, Shamma. "A Good Story Deserves Retelling--The
Unfolding of the Akiva Legend." *Jewish Studies: An Internet
Journal* 3 (2004): 55-93. www.biu.ac.il/JS/JSIJ/3-2004/
Friedman.pdf.

ARTICLE ACCESSED THROUGH AN ELECTRONIC DATABASE

To cite an article from a print journal accessed through an
electronic database, include the information you would
include for a journal article in print. Follow this by the
name of the online database; the URL; and the date of access, in parentheses, if material is time sensitive.

Toplin, Robert Brent. "The Filmmaker as Historian." *American
Historical Review* 93 (1988): 1210–27. *JSTOR.* www.jstor.org/.

ONLINE GOVERNMENT PUBLICATION

A citation for a government publication should include
the author's name, inverted, and followed by a period;
the title of the document; the type of document; the date
of publication; the URL; and the date of access, in parentheses, if the material is time sensitive.

Bush, George W. "Improving Agency Disclosure of Information."
Executive Order, December 14, 2005. www.whitehouse
.gov/news/releases/2005/12/20051214-4.html (accessed
January 3, 2006).

ONLINE NEWSPAPER ARTICLE

To cite an online newspaper article, begin with the author's last name, if known; the title of the article; the
name of the newspaper; the date of publication; the URL;
and the date of access, in parentheses, if the material is
time sensitive. All elements of the entry should be separated by periods.

Linzer, Dafna. "Strong Leads and Dead Ends in Nuclear Case
Against Iran." *WashingtonPost.com*. February 8, 2006.
www.washingtonpost.com/wp-dyn/content/article/2006/
02/07/AR2006020702126.html (accessed February 9, 2006.

ONLINE REVIEW

A citation for an online review should begin with the last
name of the reviewer; the title and author of the book
being reviewed; the name of the online publication; the
date of the review; the URL; and the date of access, in
parentheses, if the material is time sensitive. The elements of the entry should be separated by periods.

Lewis, Anthony. Review of *At Canaan's Edge: America in the King
Years, 1965-68,* by Taylor Branch. *New York Times*. February
5, 2006. www.ntimes.com/2006/02/05/books/review/
05lewis.html (accessed February 10, 2006).

WEB FORUM, LISTSERV, OR NEWSGROUP POSTING

To document a posting to a Web discussion forum, listserv, or newsgroup, include the author's name, in reverse
order; the title of the posting, in quotation marks; the
name of the list; the date of the posting; the URL; and the
date of access, in parentheses. Use periods to separate the
elements in the entry.

Gudmundson, Lowell W. "INFO: New On-Line Materials on
Afro-Central American History." E-mail to H-Net Latin
American History Forum. February 3, 2006. http://
h-net.msu.edu/cgi-bin/logbrowse.pl?trx=vx&list=H
-LatAm&month=0602 (accessed February 8, 2006).

E-MAIL MESSAGE

Since readers will not have access to your e-mail, e-mail messages do not need to be listed in your bibliography.

CD-ROM

Kline, Naomi Reed. *A Wheel of Memory: The Hereford Mappamundi*. CD-ROM. Ann Arbor: University of Michigan Press, 2001.

7e. Sample pages from a student research paper

Most of the suggestions in this book have been directed toward a single end: the production of a carefully researched, well-organized, and clearly written paper. On the following pages, you will find the title page, opening paragraphs, notes, and bibliography for one such paper.

SAMPLE TITLE PAGE

To Try a Monarch:
The Trials and Executions of
Charles I of England and Louis XVI of France

by
Lynn Chandler

History 362
Dr. Joan Kinnaird
November 22, 2006

SAMPLE PAGE

On January 30, 1649, Charles I, king of England, was be-headed.[1] The crowd around the scaffold greeted the sight of the severed head of their monarch with astonished silence. After lying in state for several days, the body was carried "in a Hearse covered with black Velvet, and drawn by six Horses, with four Coaches following it. . . ."[2] to Windsor Castle, where Charles was buried in royal estate beside Henry VIII and Queen Jane Seymour.[3] The scene was quite different on January 21, 1793, when another monarch ascended the scaffold--Louis XVI, king of the French. In place of the silence that followed Charles's execution, Louis's decapitation was announced with a "flourish of trumpets," and the executioner's cry of "Thus dies a Traitor!"[4] Contemporaries reported that the crowd surged forward, dipped their handkerchiefs in the king's blood, and ran through the streets shouting "Behold the Blood of a Tyrant!"[5] The body was wrapped in canvas and brought in a cart to the Tuileries, where Louis XVI, the former king of France, was buried like a commoner.[6] These two events, separated by almost a century and a half, appear at first glance to be totally isolated from each other. A careful review of both official documents and private accounts, however, reveals that the chief actors in the drama surrounding the execution of Louis XVI were not only aware of the English precedent, but referred to it again and again in the process of choosing their own courses of action, arguing for the validity of their point of view, and justifying their actions to the world.

The first clear-cut evidence that the French were influenced by the trial and execution of Charles I can be found in contemporary transcripts of the trial itself. In the debate surrounding the decision to execute the king, those who favored leniency often cited the English precedent to support their position.

SAMPLE ENDNOTES PAGE

Chandler 10

Notes

1. For a good general study of the execution, see Ann Hughes, "The Execution of Charles I," May 2001, www.bbc.co.uk/history/state/monarchs_leaders/charlesi_execution_01.shtml.

2. *England's Black Tribunal: The Tryal of King Charles the First* (printed for C. Revington, at the Bible and Crown in St. Paul's Churchyard, 1737), 55.

3. For a detailed account of the trial and execution of Charles I, see C. V. Wedgwood, *A Coffin for King Charles: The Trial and Execution of Charles I* (New York: Time Incorporated, 1966), and Graham Edwards, *The Last Days of Charles I* (Stroud, Gloucestershire: Sutton Publishing, 1999).

4. Joseph Trapp, *The Trial of Louis XVI* (London, 1793), 205.

5. Trapp, 206.

6. Trapp, 145. For a detailed account of the trial and execution of Louis XVI, see David P. Jordan, *The King's Trial: The French Revolution vs. Louis XVI* (Berkeley and Los Angeles: University of California Press, 1979).

7. Michael Walzer, ed., *Regicide and Revolution: Speeches at the Trial of Louis XVI,* trans. Marian Rothstein (Cambridge: Cambridge University Press, 1974), 1–89 passim.

8. Patricia Crawford, "'Charles Stuart, That Man of Blood,'" *Journal of British Studies* 16, no. 2 (1977): 53.

9. Wedgwood, 89.

10. Susan Dunn, *The Deaths of Louis XVI: Regicide and the French Political Imagination* (Princeton, NJ: Princeton University Press, 1994), 59.

11. Jordan, 122.

12. John Hardman, *The French Revolution Sourcebook* (London: Arnold Publishers, 1999), 178.

SAMPLE BIBLIOGRAPHY

Chandler 11

Bibliography

Crawford, Patricia. "'Charles Stuart, That Man of Blood.'" *Journal of British Studies* 16, no. 2 (1977): 41–61.

Dunn, Susan. *The Deaths of Louis XVI: Regicide and the French Political Imagination.* Princeton, NJ: Princeton University Press, 1994.

Edwards, Graham. *The Last Days of Charles I.* Stroud, Gloucestershire: Sutton Publishing, 1999.

England's Black Tribunal: The Tryal of King Charles the First. Printed for C. Revington, at the Bible and Crown in St. Paul's Churchyard, 1737.

Hardman, John. *The French Revolution Sourcebook.* London: Arnold Publishers, 1999.

Hughes, Ann. "The Execution of Charles I." www.bbc.co.uk/history/state/monarchs_leaders/charlesi_execution_01.shtml.

Jordan, David P. "In Defense of the King." *Stanford French Review* 1, no. 3 (1977): 325–38.

---. *The King's Trial: The French Revolution vs. Louis XVI.* Berkeley and Los Angeles: University of California Press, 1979.

Trapp, Joseph. *The Trial of Louis XVI.* London, 1793.

Walzer, Michael, ed. *Regicide and Revolution: Speeches at the Trial of Louis XVI.* Translated by Marian Rothstein. Cambridge: Cambridge University Press, 1974.

Wedgwood, C. V. *A Coffin for King Charles: The Trial and Execution of Charles I.* New York: Time Incorporated, 1966.

Appendix A ·
Writing Guides of Interest to Historians

The following books offer helpful guidance on stylistic matters and other writing concerns. The guides to writing in history, in addition to offering general advice, discuss how historians work and cover typical assignments, stylistic conventions, the research process, and documentation.

GENERAL WRITING GUIDES

Hacker, Diana. *A Pocket Style Manual.* 4th ed. Boston: Bedford/St. Martin's, 2004. Also available at www.dianahacker.com/pocket.

Strunk, William, Jr., and E. B. White. *The Elements of Style.* 4th ed. New York: Macmillan, 1999.

Turabian, Kate L., Alice Bennett, and John Grossman. *A Manual for Writers of Term Papers, Theses, and Dissertations.* 6th ed. Chicago: University of Chicago Press, 1996.

University of Chicago Press. *The Chicago Manual of Style.* 15th ed. Chicago: University of Chicago Press, 2003.

GUIDES TO WRITING IN HISTORY

Benjamin, Jules R. *A Student's Guide to History.* 10th ed. Boston: Bedford/St. Martin's, 2007. Also available at bedfordstmartins .com/benjamin.

Hellstern, Mark, Gregory M. Scott, and Stephen M. Garrison. *The History Student Writer's Manual.* Upper Saddle River, NJ: Prentice Hall, 1998.

Marius, Richard, and Melvin E. Page. *A Short Guide to Writing about History.* 5th ed. New York: Pearson Education, 2005.

Storey, William Kelleher. *Writing History: A Guide for Students.* 2nd ed. New York: Oxford University Press, 2004.

INTERNET GUIDES FOR HISTORIANS

Gevinson, Alan, Kelly Schrum, and Roy Rosenzweig. *History Matters: A Student Guide to U.S. History Online.* Boston: Bedford/St. Martin's, 2005.

Harnack, Andrew, and Eugene Kleppinger. *Online! A Reference Guide to Using Internet Sources.* 3rd ed. Boston: Bedford/St. Martin's, 2003. Also available at bedfordstmartins.com/online.

Reagan, Patrick. *Guide to History and the Internet.* Boston: McGraw-Hill, 2002.

Trinkle, Dennis A., and Scott A. Merriman. *The European History Highway: A Guide to Internet Resources.* Armonk, NY: M. E. Sharpe. 2002.

Trinkle, Dennis A., and Scott A. Merriman. *The History Highway 3.0: A Guide to Internet Resources.* 3rd ed. Armonk, NY: M. E. Sharpe, 2002.

· Appendix B
Selected Print and Online Resources in History

by Susan Craig, Valencia Community College

While doing research in history, you will need to collect evidence and find commentary that helps you interpret it. Your library and the Internet offer many tools that can help you track down primary and secondary sources and answer questions that arise as you learn more about your topic. This appendix lists selected encyclopedias, dictionaries, indexes, and guides as well as a sampling of electronic research resources available through the Internet. Some electronic databases and archives are available by subscription only; check with your local public or academic library for access.

Library resources

The materials listed here are not available at all libraries, but they give you an idea of the range of resources available. Remember, too, that librarians are an extremely helpful resource. They know their own collections well and can direct you to useful materials throughout your research process.

OVERVIEWS AND ENCYCLOPEDIAS

The Americas

Africana: The Encyclopedia of the African and African American Experience. 2nd ed. New York: Oxford University Press, 2005.

> This five-volume set covers African American history and culture from origins in Africa to the present-day United States and the rest of the Americas. Includes a chronology, maps, illustrations, bibliographies, and an index.

Encyclopedia Latina: History, Culture, and Society in the United States. Danbury, CT: Grolier Academic Reference, 2005.

> Over 650 topical and biographical articles in this four-volume set cover U.S.-Latino history from the sixteenth century to the present. Includes photographs, maps, appendixes, Web resources, bibliographies, and an index.

Harvard Guide to African-American History. Cambridge, MA: Harvard University Press, 2001.

Provides selected lists of the important publications in African American history in sections such as historical research and methods, comprehensive histories, and histories of special subjects. Includes an index and a CD-ROM.

Mexico: An Encyclopedia of Contemporary Culture and History. Santa Barbara, CA: ABC-CLIO, 2004.

An overview of twentieth and twenty-first century Mexico, exploring the political, economic, social, and cultural history. Includes maps, illustrations, bibliographies, and an index.

Native American Encyclopedia: History, Culture, and Peoples. New York: Oxford University Press, 2000.

Addresses over 200 Native American groups in Canada and the United States. Includes illustrations, pronunciation guide, maps, glossary, bibliographies, and an index.

The War That Made America: A Short History of the French and Indian War. New York: Viking, 2005.

A concise introduction to the war that led to eventual conflict between Britain and the American colonies. Includes maps, illustrations, bibliography, and an index.

Worldwide

Berkshire Encyclopedia of World History. Great Barrington, MA: Berkshire Publishing Group, 2005.

This five-volume set covers 250,000 years and offers 550 articles that trace the development of human history and show connections, interactions, and change over time and place. Includes illustrations, maps, topical guides, sidebars, bibliographies, and an index.

Britain and the Americas: Culture, Politics, and History: A Multidisciplinary Encyclopedia. Santa Barbara, CA: ABC-CLIO, 2005.

A three-volume set that examines Britain's cultural, political, and historical legacy to the nations of the Americas. Includes a chronology, cross-references, bibliographies, illustrations, and an index.

China: Its History and Culture. 4th ed. New York: McGraw-Hill, 2005.

Covers the origins and early history of China through the early twenty-first century. Includes maps, illustrations, bibliographies, and an index.

Columbia Guide to the Holocaust. New York: Columbia University Press, 2000.

A guide to the general history, core issues, and debates of the Holocaust. Includes maps, tables, references, online resources, and an index.

Encyclopedia of African History and Culture. New York: Facts on File, 2005.

A comprehensive five-volume encyclopedia, with each volume devoted to a major period in the continent's development from ancient times to South Africa's first democratic election in 1994. Includes illustrations, maps, references, and an index.

Encyclopedia of Islam and the Muslim World. New York: Macmillan Reference USA, 2003.

This two-volume multidisciplinary set covers Islamic life, history, geography, sociology, politics, philosophy, and religion. Includes illustrations, maps, bibliographies, cross-references, and an index. Also available as an e-book by subscription at select libraries.

Encyclopedia of Russian History. New York: Macmillan Reference USA, 2004.

This multidisciplinary four-volume encyclopedia discusses Russia's people, politics, economics, religion, and social systems from its earliest history to the rise and fall of the Soviet Union. Includes photos, maps, illustrations, references, and an index.

Encyclopedia of the Modern Middle East and North Africa. 2nd ed. Detroit: Macmillan Reference USA, 2004.

A four-volume set that covers the history of each country from a variety of perspectives including history, anthropology, economics, religion, politics, and social issues. Offers maps, illustrations, topical outlines, genealogies, glossary, bibliographies, cross references, and an index. Also available as an e-book by subscription at select libraries.

Encyclopedia of the Palestinians. Rev. ed. New York: Facts on File, 2005.

Includes illustrations, maps, bibliographies, and an index.

Encyclopedia of the Renaissance and the Reformation. Rev. ed. New York: Facts on File, 2004.

Covers thirteenth, fourteenth, and fifteenth centuries in this time of transition that defined the shape of modern western civilizations. Includes chronology, bibliographies, maps, illustrations, and an index.

Encyclopedia of the Victorian Era. Danbury, CT: Grolier Academic Reference, 2004.

This four-volume set spans 1837 to 1901. Includes maps, illustrations, chronology, bibliographies, and an index.

Encyclopedia of Wars. New York: Facts on File, 2005.

This three-volume set describes the military aspects of wars from 3500 BCE to the present as well as the social and political context in which the wars occurred. Includes maps, cross references, a chronology, a bibliography, suggestions for further reading, and an index.

A History of Japan. Malden, MA: Blackwell, 2005.

> Covers Japanese history from 400 BCE to the present. Includes illustrations, maps, references, and an index.

A History of the Ancient Near East, c. 3000–323 BC. Malden, MA: Blackwell, 2004.

> A concise narrative history. Includes bibliographies, illustrations, charts, maps, a selection of Near Eastern texts in translation, and an index.

Korea's Place in the Sun: A Modern History. New York: Norton, 2005.

> Covers Korean history from 1860 to the present. Includes maps, illustrations, references, and an index.

Middle East. 10th ed. Washington, DC: CQ Press, 2005.

> An overview of the Middle East covering the Arab-Israeli conflict, U.S. policy, the Persian Gulf, oil, Islam, and country profiles. The new edition covers the attacks of September 11, 2001, the wars in Afghanistan and Iraq, and the role of militant Islamic groups. Includes maps, tables, documents, an index, and a chronology.

New History of India. 7th ed. New York: Oxford University Press, 2004.

> Condenses 4000 years of Indian history. Includes maps, illustrations, references, and an index.

Notable Last Facts — A Compendium of Endings, Conclusions, Terminations, and Final Events throughout History. Haddonfield, NJ: Reference Desk Press, 2005.

> A "notable last" is any historically significant event, person, place, or thing that marks the end of its kind or its era, such as the last surviving witness to a historic event or the last journey of a ship or aircraft. Organized by major topics and includes bibliographies, Web resources, and an index.

Oxford History of Britain. Rev. ed. Oxford: Oxford University Press, 2001.

> A revised edition covering over 2000 years of British history, with entries in chronological order. Includes maps, illustrations, genealogy, bibliographies, and an index.

South Asia: A Historical Narrative. New York: Oxford University Press, 2003.

> Covers the evolution of the term *India* and the dawn of Indian civilization to nationalism. Includes maps, references, and an index.

Term Paper Resource Guide to Twentieth-Century World History. Westport, CT: Greenwood Press, 2000.

> Lists 100 important events in twentieth century world history from the first manned flight in 1903 to the Chinese economy at the end of the century, with a brief narrative, major issues, term paper suggestions, primary and secondary sources, and websites. Includes an index.

TOPICAL DICTIONARIES
The Americas

Dictionary of American History. 3rd ed. New York: Scribner, 2003.

This completely revised ten-volume set of terms, places, and concepts in U.S. history adds gender, race, and social-history perspectives to many entries. Includes maps, illustrations, a learning guide, and an index.

Historical Dictionary of the American Revolution. Lanham, MD: Scarecrow Press, 1999.

Includes concise topical entries, an extensive bibliography, and a collection of important military and political documents associated with the American Revolution.

The Middle East and the United States: A Historical and Political Reassessment. 3rd ed. Boulder, CO: Westview Press, 2003.

Provides perspectives on American foreign policy in the Middle East and on the Middle East in general. Updated to include new chapters on Turkey, Afghanistan, the Arab-Israeli conflict, and the successive crises in the Persian Gulf. Includes bibliographies and an index.

Worldwide

Cassell's Dictionary of Modern German History. London: Cassell, 2002.

Covers 250 years of modern German history from 1700 through the twentieth century, dealing with political, social, economic, military, and cultural events. Includes references and a chronology.

Dictionary of the Israeli-Palestinian Conflict: Culture, History, and Politics. Farmington Hills, MI: Thomson Gale, 2005.

A two-volume set covering the history of the conflict from the birth of Zionism in 1897 to 2004. Includes cross references, images, maps, and bibliographies. Also available as an e-book by subscription at select libraries.

Dictionary of the Middle Ages. New York: Scribner, 1982–89; 2003 supplement.

The single most complete source covering people, events, ideas, movements, texts, and cultural features of the medieval world. The thirteen-volume set covers AD 500 to AD 1500. The supplement volume adds over 320 topics to broaden and update the coverage, adding more detail on women and gender issues, numerous first-time biographies, and new scholarship on social issues.

Historical Dictionary of Iraq. Lanham, MD: Scarecrow Press, 2004.

Covers Iraq's history from Mesopotamia to the present, with personalities (from Hammurabi to Saddam Hussein) and significant places. Includes a chronology, maps, tribal breakdowns, and topical appendices.

Historical Dictionary of the Republic of Korea. 2nd ed. Lanham, MD: Scarecrow Press, 2004.

Hundreds of entries describe the people, political and social events, foreign affairs, and economic and cultural developments that have shaped South Korea since its creation in 1948. Includes a chronology, maps, and topical appendices.

Oxford Dictionary of National Biography: In Association with the British Academy. From the Earliest Times to the Year 2000. Oxford: Oxford University Press, 2004.

A 61-volume revised edition of the *Dictionary of National Biography,* 1885–1901. Provides 50,000 biographies of men and women who shaped the British path over the past 2400 years, with over 36,000 newly written biographies, 13,500 newly selected people, and 3,000 biographies of women. Covers the British Isles, Britons abroad, and former colonies. Includes portrait illustrations and an index volume of contributors. Also available online by subscription at select libraries.

ATLASES, CHRONOLOGIES, AND TIMETABLES

The Americas

African American Years. New York: Scribner, 2003.

A chronology of African American history from colonial times to the end of the twentieth century. Includes maps, illustrations, a bibliography, and an index. Also available as an e-book by subscription at select libraries.

Atlas of American History. Revised ed. New York: Facts on File, 2006.

Covers American history from prehistory to the war on terror, including military, migration, social, and religious history. Aligned with the *National Standards for United States History.* Integrates maps with text and includes illustrations, photographs, charts, graphs, and an index.

Atlas of Hispanic-American History. New York: Facts on File, 2001.

An overview of important events surrounding Hispanic Americans of North, South, and Central America. Includes photographs, maps, a bibliography, and an index.

Atlas of Asian American History. New York: Checkmark Books, 2002.

Offers an in-depth look at the political and social history of Asian Americans. Includes photographs, maps, charts, a bibliography, and an index.

Worldwide

Cassell's Chronology of World History: Dates, Events, and Ideas That Made History. London: Weidenfeld & Nicolson, 2005.

A summary of world history, offering essays on events, peoples, and themes.

Chambers History Factfinder. Edinburgh, Scotland: Chambers, 2005.

A chronology of world events, including timelines and numerous lists such as battles, famous last words, presidents, and strange laws of the past.

Concise Atlas of the World. 6th ed. New York: Oxford University Press, 2002.

Traces 12,000 years of history, with coverage of all areas. Includes maps, illustrations, tables, cross-references, and an index.

Historical Atlas of Empires: From 4000 BC to the 21st Century. London: Mercury Books, 2004.

Spanning 6000 years, this atlas "shows that our modern global society is the direct result of accumulated effects of the empires of yesteryear." Includes maps, timelines, illustrations, and an index.

Key Events in African History: A Reference Guide. Westport, CT: Greenwood, 2002.

A guide to African history from ancient times to Nelson Mandela's government. Includes illustrations and maps. Also available as an e-book by subscription at select libraries.

Penguin Atlas of World History. Updated ed. London: Penguin, 2003.

A two-volume chronological summary of the main cultural, scientific, religious, and political events from the beginning of world history to 2001.

Routledge Atlas of British History: from 45 BC to the Present Day. 3rd ed. London: Routledge, 2003.

Charts the history of Britain as well as social, economic, political, and religious perspectives throughout history. Includes updated maps.

World Leaders of the Twentieth Century. Pasadena, CA: The Press, 2000.

Two-volume set offers biographies of heads of state and political leaders from Konrad Adenauer to Boris Yeltsin. Includes a bibliography and an index. Also available as an e-book by subscription at select libraries.

Internet Resources

The Internet is an important research tool and is an increasingly useful place to find primary sources. You can view photographs and drawings, play audio recordings of speeches or U.S. Supreme Court arguments, or find historical documents that you can print or save to your own computer. As you use the Internet for research, be sure to assess the value of the material you find (see 2b-3) and to document where you found it (see 7b-3). The websites listed represent only a sampling of the extensive history sources available. For guides to using the Internet for historical research, see Appendix A.

SEARCH ENGINES AND DIRECTORIES

Search engines are programs that locate Internet sources containing the search terms that you provide. Because they seek matches based exclusively on the words you enter and don't screen for quality, they may produce vast numbers of irrelevant or useless results. They work best when you have a fairly specific topic and when you use search techniques such as Boolean operators and phrase searching with quotation marks.

Google. www.google.com

> Allows basic, advanced, and image searching, and much more. Includes limited search directory features; click on more», then click on Directory, Society, and History.

MetaCrawler. www.metacrawler.com

> Searches leading search engines. Offers basic and advanced searching plus images and audio.

Ask. com. http://search.ask.com

> *Ask.com* has merged with *Teoma.com* to create a powerful search engine. Allows basic and advanced searching. Results often offer suggestions to help you narrow or expand your search.

Search directories list Internet sites organized by subject, with some level of evaluation. A good directory may lead to information more quickly than a search engine, especially if your topic is fairly broad. Directories return a smaller but more selective set of results than do search engines.

Librarian's Index to the Internet. www.lii.org

> Indexes history under "Arts & Humanities."

Open Directory Project. http://dmoz.com

> Indexes history under "Society."

GENERAL HISTORY INTERNET SITES

Best of History Web Sites. www.besthistorysites.net

> Contains annotated links to over 1000 history websites.

eHistory. http://ehistory.osu.edu

> Offers over 130,000 pages of historical content; 5,300 timeline events; 800 battle outlines; 350 biographies; and thousands of images and maps.

History World. www.historyworld.net

This interactive site contains over 400 historical narratives and descriptions of over 6,000 world events, with an emphasis on English history. Includes timelines and an online game where visitors can pit their historical knowledge against that of other competitors.

HistoryNet. www.historynet.com

This site features a searchable, full-text archive of articles from ten magazines published by the Primedia History Group, including *American History, British Heritage, Military History,* and *Wild West.* Also features a today-in-history list of events and a picture of the day with a related article.

Internet Public Library — History. www.ipl.org/div/subject/browse/hum30.00.00

Provides history links by region, era, topic, documents, and sources.

Repositories of Primary Sources. www.uidaho.edu/special-collections/Other.Repositories.html

Lists over 5,000 websites describing holdings of manuscripts, archives, rare books, historical photographs, and other primary sources.

SPECIALIZED SITES FOR HISTORICAL RESEARCH

North America

AMDOCS. www.ku.edu/carrie/docs/amdocs_index.html#1787

Primary source documents for the study of American history from 1492 to 2005.

American Memory. http://memory.loc.gov/ammem/amhome.html

Over 130 multimedia collections of digitized documents, photographs, recorded sound, moving pictures, and text highlighting important American historical events; from the Library of Congress.

American Periodicals Series Online. First release 1741–1800. Ann Arbor: ProQuest Information and Learning Company, 2000–.

A growing full-text collection of American magazines and journals derived from the *American Periodicals Series* microform collection. *APS Online* features digitized images of articles from over 1,100 periodicals, including scholarly, scientific, and popular magazines and journals. This database is a work in progress and does not yet include all the *APS* content. It is available by subscription only at select libraries.

American Social History Project. www.ashp.cuny.edu

Offers print, visual, multimedia, and online resources in American history.

Congressional Record. Washington, DC: GPO, 1873–.

Covers debates and proceedings of Congress. Earlier series were called *Debates and Proceedings* (generally known as *An-*

nals of Congress (1789–1824), Register of Debates (1824–1837), and *Congressional Globe (1833–1873).* Also available on microfilm, CD-ROM, and online from 1994 onward via http://www.gpoaccess.gov/crecord/index.html.

Documenting the American South. http://docsouth.unc edu/about

Digitized primary materials that offer Southern perspectives on American history and culture.

Documents from the Women's Liberation Movement. http://scriptorium.lib.duke.edu/wlm

An online archival collection of documents from the late 1960s to the early 1970s.

Foreign Relations of the United States. Diplomatic Papers. Washington, DC: GPO, 1861–.

A collection of documents including diplomatic papers, correspondence, and memoranda that provides a detailed record of U.S. foreign policy. Some documents are available online from the Truman to the Nixon and Ford administrations at http://www.state.gov/r/pa/ho/frus.

History Matters: U.S. History Survey Course. http://historymatters .gmu.edu

This gateway to Web resources offers primary documents, strategies for analyzing online primary material, and an annotated guide to over 800 websites on American history.

Library of Congress. www.loc.gov

The website for the largest library in the world includes the American Memory Project, Global Gateway to World Culture and Resources, and current historical legislative information.

Making of America. http://cdl.library.cornell.edu/moa

Primary sources in American social history from the antebellum period through reconstruction.

Slave Narratives from the Federal Writers' Project, 1936–1938. http://lcweb2.loc.gov/ammem/snhtml

Contains more than 2,300 first-person accounts of slavery and 500 photographs of former slaves.

Worldwide

BBC Learning: History. www.bbc.co.uk/learning/subjects/history .shtml

Offers links to history resources from the BBC website and from the Web.

Internet Modern History Sourcebook. www.fordham.edu/halsall/ mod/modsbook.html

A history primary sourcebook that offers websites for teachers and students in college survey courses in American and European modern history.

EuroDocs: Primary Historical Documents from Western Europe. http://library.byu.edu/~rdh/eurodocs

Provides links to Western European documents (mainly primary sources), organized by country and period.

Hansard's Parliamentary Debates. Great Britain. www.publications
.parliament.uk/pa/cm/cmhansrd.htm

Proceedings of the British Parliament, with the text of debates
in the House of Commons and the House of Lords. The full
text of many debates from 1988 to the present is available.

History News Network. http://hnn.us/

Offers articles by historians putting the news in perspective
on a daily basis.

NetSERF: The Internet Connection to Medieval Resources. www
.netserf.org

Links to sites on various aspects of medieval life, including
history, arts, culture, literature, music, religion, and women.
Includes a "research center" with an extensive glossary.

ORB: Online Reference Book for Medieval Studies. www.the-orb.net

Written and maintained by medieval scholars, this site offers
an encyclopedia, online texts, resources for teaching, and
links to other online resources.

Portals to the World. www.loc.gov/rr/international/portals.html

From the Library of Congress, this site provides links to
electronic resources from around the world, with country
information on history, politics, culture, business, and
travel.

A Teacher's Guide to the Holocaust. http://fcit.usf.edu/holocaust

Provides an overview of the people and events of the Holocaust through photographs, documents, art, music, movies,
and literature. Includes teacher resources.

WWW Virtual Library: History. http://vlib.org/History

Provides links to history resources organized by subject areas.

DIRECTORIES TO ELECTRONIC LIBRARY CATALOGS

LibDex. www.libdex.com

A worldwide directory of online library catalogs. Browse the
index by country or by library name.

LibWeb. http://sunsite.berkeley.edu/Libweb

Lists online library servers, searchable by name, type, or
country.

JOURNAL INDEXES

An increasing number of periodicals are available in electronic format on the Internet. Some titles offer online access to entire issues, others provide access to selective
articles, and others just list citations to the articles. Your
library may subscribe to electronic versions of print journals and online periodical databases (such as *ProQuest*,
EBSCO*Host*, *FirstSearch*, *JSTOR*, or *Project Muse*), making

them available through the Internet with appropriate password authentication.

America: History and Life. Santa Barbara, CA: ABC-CLIO, 1964–.

> Abstracts of articles on the history of the United States and Canada published throughout the world, as well as articles dealing with current U.S. culture. Includes book reviews and abstracts of dissertations. Available at subscribing libraries in print and online formats.

FirstSearch. Dublin, OH: OCLC www.oclc.org/firstsearch

> This online service provides indexing and full-text articles (over 10 million) from dozens of subject databases. Information on the product is available at the link, but searching is only available at subscribing libraries. Underlying *FirstSearch* is *WorldCat,* the world's largest database of items held in libraries.

Historical Abstracts. Santa Barbara, CA: ABC-CLIO, 1955–.

> Abstracts from periodical literature covering world history from 1450. The scope excludes the United States and Canada. From 1971, selectively indexes book reviews, monographs, and dissertations as well as periodical literature. Also available in print.

Humanities Index. New York: H. W. Wilson, 1974–.

> An index to international magazines and journals in the field of humanities, including history. From 1907 to 1974, this index was in a combined title, *Social Sciences and Humanities Index.* Also available in print.

JSTOR: The Scholarly Journal Archive. New York: JSTOR User Services www.jstor.org

> This online service for archiving academic journals provides indexing and full-text articles from several hundred journals, some going as far back as the 1600s. *JSTOR* does not offer access to the most recent issues of journals. Available by subscription at select libraries.

Project Muse. http://muse.jhu.edu

> Provides online access to over 300 journals in the humanities, arts, and social sciences. Indexing to article citations is available free at the above link. Online full-text articles are available at subscribing libraries and through interlibrary loan. *Project Muse* keeps an archive of its journals once they go online but does not have issues that predate them. In many cases, older articles are still useful, and students will need to find them by using print indexes.

ELECTRONIC JOURNALS AND MAGAZINES

These are a few sites to help you locate free online periodicals and newspapers:

Directory of Open Access Journals. www.doaj.org/home

Offers access to over 2000 full-text journals, with 500 journals searchable at the article level. Search for topical articles from the home page or browse the list of history journals at http://www.doaj.org/ljbs?cpid=13.

Newspaper Directories. www.libdex.com/newspapers.html

Links to over twenty worldwide newspaper websites.

Internet Public Library Newspapers. www.ipl.org/div/news

Lists online newspapers from around the world.

History Journals Guide. www.history-journals.de

Lists hundreds of e-journals with articles available online; select a journal title and search the table of contents for available online content.

ORGANIZATIONS

American Historical Association. www.historians.org

H-Net. www.h-net.org

An international interdisciplinary organization of scholars and teachers that offers discussion networks in a wide variety of fields of historical study as well as the Matrix, a multimedia research center. For links to the electronic discussion lists maintained by *H-Net,* go to www.h-net.org/lists.

Oral History Association. http://omega.dickinson.edu/organizations/oha

Organization of American Historians. www.oah.org

Index

Directory to Documentation Models